MW01659629

WHAT GOT YOU WHERE YOU ARE TODAY?

BY

IRIS ACKER

dp
DISTINCTIVE PUBLISHING CORP.

WHAT GOT YOU WHERE YOU ARE TODAY?
By Iris Y. Acker

Produced by Ratzlaff & Associates
Cover and Illustrations by Therese Cabell
Published by Distinctive Publishing Corp.
P.O. Box 17868
Plantation, FL 33318-7868

Printed in the United States of America
ISBN: 0-942963-08-3
Library of Congress No. 90-86069
Price $12.95

Celebrities For

WHAT GOT YOU WHERE YOU ARE TODAY

MORE WISE WORDS FROM THE STARS

TO THE READER

I've been in and out of professional theater since I was eleven years old and have had the good fortune to "support" many, many stars in plays in New York, in "Summer Stock," on tour and in regional theaters.

I nearly wrote a book I was going to call 'Stars I Have Supported,' or 'How Did They Ever Stand Up Without Me?' One thing that's never changed for me, I'm still "Star Struck."

For the past six years, I've produced and hosted *On Stage With Iris Acker* on WLRN, Public Television in Miami, and interviewed some of the most respected celebrities to grace the stages of our theaters, film screens and television sets.

Because I really wanted to know the answer to "What Got You Where You Are Today?" I found myself including the question in all my interviews. In reviewing the tapes of my past programs, I found the responses extremely educational. Each celebrity "made it" in a different way. This encouraged me to compile and select my favorites for this book.

The performers' willingness to share their successes and failures, to advise those just starting out, while revealing what they'd do if they could start all over again, will endear them to you, as they have to me.

THANK YOU

Celeste Bennett

Linda Bryant

Carla Cold

Bob Di Stolfi

Woody Graber

Silvia Michelena

Nancy Richards

Joy Reese Shaw

Karen Vock

Sharmila Vooraklcara

Martin Yoffe

Lee Zimmerman

ABOUT THE AUTHOR

IRIS ACKER

Representative Theatre:

In New York: Mrs. Holly in *Suddenly Last Summer*, Mrs. Mullin in *Carousel*, The Widow in *A Box Of Tears*, Mrs. Puffy in *The Streets Of New York*, Helen in *A Taste Of Honey*, Madame Elizabeth in *Look Homeward Angel*, Amanda in *The Glass Menagerie*.

In Florida: *Almost Perfect*, *Social Security*, *Grease*, and *Norman Is That You* at The Burt Reynolds Jupiter Theatre, *Night Of The Iguana*, at the Tennessee Williams Fine Arts Center, *Tribute* and *Marriage Go Round* at The Alhambra, Jacksonville, FL; *Last Of The Red Hot Lovers* at Coconut Grove Playhouse, FL.

In Regional & Touring Theatres: *The Royal Family*, *Come Blow Your Horn*, *A Visit To A Small Planet*, *Minnie's Boys*, *The Gingerbread Lady*, *Plaza Suite*, *Lovers And Other Strangers*, *Isn't It Romantic*, *Fiddler On The Roof*, *The Subject Was Roses*, *A Shot In The Dark*, *Any Wednesday*, *Let's Hear It For Miss America*, *Gypsy*.

Recent Films and TV: *Cocoon II*, *Intimate Strangers*, *Flight Of The Navigator*, *Whoops Apocalypse*, *The Unholy*, *Gift Of The Maji*, *The Pilot*, *Wiseguy* and *Doubles*.

Iris was nominated twice for Carbonnel Theatre Awards: for *Social Security* at the Burt Reynolds Jupiter Theatre and for *Lovers And Other Strangers*. Two years in a row she won

"Women Who Make A Difference" awarded by the Florida Y.W.C.A., both times for her TV program *On Stage With Iris Acker* which she hosts and produces for Public Television.

The Florida Bar gave an award to Iris for producing the program *The Jury Box*, and The National Council of Jewish Women awarded her with their annual "Women In Power" award.

IRIS ACKER

GEORGE ABBOTT

"Acting is just being the character. All acting is, as Shakespeare said, just hold the mirror up to nature."

George Abbott

I was a pretty good actor in high school and college . . . but I always wanted to be a writer. At the University of Rochester, I wrote a play for the drama class and, of course, wrote the best part for myself.

After school, I wrote a play with my friend Jimmy Gleason. We were going to direct together, but he got a big part in something else, so I got to direct for the first time.

My first musical "break" was an offer to direct and collaborate on *On Your Toes.* Since I'd never directed a musical before, they offered me *Jumbo* to get my feet wet. That's when I fell in love with musicals.

I've had many successes, but I've also had failures. A musical called *Music Is* had a lot of reasons for failing, but we found out too late. The play *Broadway* was done very successfully in Cleveland recently, so we took it to New York . . . and it failed.

Finding the right actor for the part is so rewarding. When I write I have a "character" in mind; not a particular actor, except with *Where's Charley*, which I wrote for Ray Bolger.

To find the right actor we must hold auditions, which is comparatively new in theater. We used to interview in the office, hire them, then fire them if they weren't any good. Now, of course, with auditions, we seldom have to change anyone . . . but I realize it's a terrible strain on the actor to get out there and look out and see all these antagonistic creatures saying, "Be good, I dare you!"

Yet we do think, "I hope he's good." You get so excited when you discover someone. If only they didn't do so many wrong things when they audition. Somebody, in some drama school, has convinced them they have to get in the mood, so they take too much time going into deep thought. Just say, "Here I am, and this is what I can do." If you're prepared, you can just do it.

I teach, by directing. The director has a picture in his mind and must convey it to get the character. Acting, after all, is just being the character. All acting is, as Shakespeare said, just ". . . hold the mirror up to nature."

I always fall in love with what I'm working on. I've been cursed all my life with the need to write. This year, my 102nd, I'd like to have the play I just wrote produced. I don't care where. Just to do it, one more time.

NOTE: The musical play *Frankie* written and directed by George Abbott, ran from October 6–29, 1989, at The York Theatre in New York City.

GEORGE ABBOTT

Mr. Abbott was 103 on June 25, 1990. He has won six Tony awards; The Pulitzer Prize for *Fiorello*, and The Kennedy Center Lifetime Achievement Award.

As an actor he appeared in *The Queen's Enemy!*

As an assistant stage manager: *Three Wise Fools.*

Co-author and director: *Love Em and Leave Em.*

Directed: *Too Many Girls; Coquette; Four Walls; Three Men On A Horse; On Your Toes; The Boys From Syracuse; Best Foot Forward; Where's Charley; A Tree Grows In Brooklyn; The Pajama Game; Damn Yankees; New Girl In Town; Chicago; Boy Meets Girl; Brother Rat; Room Service; What A Life; Primrose Path; Pal Joey; Kiss And Tell; On The Town; Billion Dollar Baby; High Button Shoes; Call Me Madam; Wonderful Town; Never Too Late; A Funny Thing Happened On The Way To The Forum; Take Her, She's Mine; Flora, The Red Menace; Fade Out — Fade In; Help Stamp Out Marriage; Agatha Sue, I Love You; How Now, Dow Jones; The Education Of Hyman Kaplan; The Fig Leaves Are Falling; Norman, Is That You; Not Now Darling.*

DESI ARNAZ, JR.

When I'm asked, "How do I get into show business?", I ask, "Do you want to act or do you want to be famous?"

Desi Arnaz, Jr.

I grew up with the kid who played Little Ricky on *I Love Lucy* on TV, and I was born the same day he was. They filmed the show four months before I was born and had decided it was going to be a boy on the show. It was just a coincidence that I was.

They wanted a kid who could play drums. They found him playing with Lionel Hampton and Horace Heidt when he was three years old. We became best friends and I played the drums, too. When I was six years old, we had a Dixie Land Band and played on the *Dinah Shore Show*. When I was ten, I was with a Rock and Roll band called "The Jaguars." We sang like "The Four Seasons." Before I was thirteen, I was a member of the hit-producing rock musical trio, "Dino, Desi and Billy." That's when I started performing musically. When I was fifteen, I really started to work. I was on *Here's Lucy* with my mother and my sister.

The only "drama" training I had was in high school, but I think I inherited my talent as well as learning from my mother and father. I watched them and worked with them, growing up on TV. I think my parents were very talented and they did a good job. They were really funny, those two. Now, my timing is not like my mother's, although there is some sense of the same. But it wasn't just my parents I learned from. I grew up with Dean Martin and Frank Sinatra and their kids. I remember Buddy Hackett and Milton Berle coming to the house. We learn from a lot of different sources.

I've taken singing lessons, after rock and roll, for which I didn't have any real training. I studied with David Craig, who is one of the few who teaches you to act a song. Since he's not a voice teacher, I studied singing with another interesting teacher. He's a Cantor at a Temple, like the original *Jazz Singer*, a Cantor who's gone into show business, teaching voice and producing rock and roll shows.

A lot happened to me in the last few years. I became intrigued with what life is really about. I wondered who I was from a very early age, when people kept asking me if I was "Little Ricky." So, my whole life has kind of been a search for, "What on earth am I really doing here?" Since I grew up in show business, I saw what really didn't work at a very early age. I found life has a much greater significance for human beings. So I decided to stop doing what was hurting me. I went through a whole stage of my life with a serious problem with drugs and alcohol. I saw that was just the tip of the iceberg. That drugs weren't actually the problem at all, but only a deadly effect of an even greater problem, which is what life is really about; lack of understanding.

I've been involved in a program, "Life Without Stress," which is not a drug program. It's for all people. You have to get involved in a good drug program first. You learn to walk away from all types of self-defeating behavior. Feeling bad, anger, fear and worry. It's a re-conditioning of what life is all about, and to learn to be a happy, healthy human being.

What I found is, if you're going to be an actor, you should do it because you want to do it. When I'm asked, "How do I get into show business?", I ask, "Do you want to act or do you want to be famous?" I think acting is blown out of proportion. People should just be able to enjoy it. Once more . . . "Life without stress" . . . happy, healthy human beings.

DESI ARNAZ, JR.

Very few actors, past or future, can make this claim — but when Desi Arnaz, Jr., was born, the public and critics alike gave him rave reviews. And they haven't stopped since. Before he was thirteen years old, Desi was well on his way to becoming a seasoned entertainer as a member of the hit-producing musical rock trio, "Dino, Desi and Billy."

And that was just the beginning. After starring with his mother and sister in his mother's phenomenal hit show, *Here's Lucy*, Desi branched out into major motion pictures. In 1970, after receiving wide critical acclaim for his starring role in Hal Wallis' classic *Red Sky At Morning*, Desi received the prestigious Golden Globe Award for the Most Promising

Newcomer. Success breeds success and in 1972 Desi shared star billing with Gregory Peck in Norman Jewison's award-winning film, *Billy Two Hats.* In 1973, with Zero Mostel, he appeared in the feature musical film, *Marco Polo.* More feature films followed, including over 20 movies for television.

Meanwhile, on stage, Desi continued to attract critical attention. In 1976 he starred with Linda Day George for the John Kenley Players performing William Inge's popular *Sunday In New York.* When Desi did *Grease* with co-star Linda Purl at the Sacramento Music Center in 1980, critics glowed and called him "an experience not to be missed, a 'star name' who earns his money." After one season in 1983 with his own television series *Automan*, Desi returned to the theatre in Neil Simon's *Promises, Promises* at the Melody Top Theatre. He reprised this role again the following year at the Sacramento Music Circus. He played Alvin in *I Love My Wife* at the Coconut Grove Playhouse. Today, Mr. Desi Arnaz, Jr., is busier than ever.

PHILIP ASTOR

"Even the bad things will teach you what not to do."

Philip Astor

I trained at Illinois Wesleyan University in Drama, Speech and English literature. Then I was very fortunate, I went to the Yale Drama School. There was a great acting coach who taught there for nearly fifty years. Her name was Constance Welch. She taught Judy Holliday, Julie Harris and Paul Newman. There's not a day goes by, where as an actor, director or coach, that I don't use what Miss Welch gave me. One of those fortunate things in your life, when you come in contact with that one person, that does everything for you.

After Yale, I went to the Studio Arena Theatre in Buffalo, New York. I worked there for two solid seasons. In the summer, Williamstown Theatre Festival.

My first Broadway Show was *1776*. I got cast from an Actors Equity "open call" without an agent. I had worked with Peter Hunt, the director, and after five auditions, got the part, along with twenty-six other actors. We were mostly repertory actors, and as many as two-thirds of the cast made their Broadway debut, on March 15, 1969. I was twenty-three years old at the time.

I replaced Harvey Fierstein in *Torch Song Trilogy* and played the role of Arnold Beckoff, your typical Jewish boy from Brooklyn, who just happens to be a "drag queen" by occupation, for twenty-two months.

I turned down the San Francisco company offer for matinees only, when I was nearly broke. I was skating on very thin ice, but two months later, the Broadway offer came. I learned the script in seven days and opened in twelve days. The hardest thing I had to learn was how to crochet, which the character must do. I kept thinking . . . if Grandma could see me now, she'd never believe it.

Now, I go back and forth between acting and directing, and learn enormous things from the actors. I go to see anybody in any play. Even the bad things will teach you what not to do.

If you can't go to Yale, keep your wits about you, use common sense, watch people, and train and work wherever and whenever you can.

PHILIP ASTOR

Philip starred on Broadway as Arnold Beckoff in *Torch Song Trilogy* for two years. He was a member of the original Broadway casts of *1776, Nuts,* and *All Over Town* directed by Dustin Hoffman. Off-Broadway he originated the role of Guy in *In The Boom Boom Room* at the Public Theatre. Also, for Joseph Papp he appeared in *Trolius And Cressida* at Lincoln Center and *As You Like It* in Central Park. At the famous Williamstown Theatre Festival, he has appeared in 14 productions.

He also played Hysterium in *A Funny Thing Happened On The Way To The Forum*, Harry Roat in *Wait Until Dark*, and Phil Romano in *That Championship Season*, among many others. Philip recently completed a four-month run as Johnny in *Frankie and Johnny In Clair De Lune* at the Encore Room Theatre of the Coconut Grove Playhouse. On the Coconut Grove Playhouse mainstage, he appeared as "good old" Lenny, Lino, the Punk, Uncle Fausto and Barbara Vonelli in *The Rink*, and as Mullcady in *The Hostage*.

He had running roles on *Search For Tomorrow*, *Another World*, and *As The World Turns*. Film appearances include *Sunday Dinner* opposite Maureen Stapleton, and Max, the meanest casting director in New York in *Walls Of Glass,* which starred Geraldine Page. He recently completed filming a scene opposite Bette Midler in *Stella Dallas*.

Phillip is an adjunct professor at the University of Miami School of Music, where he teaches acting and directs the Musical Theatre Workshop. He is a native of New Jersey, lived in Manhattan for 19 years, and relocated to Coconut Grove, Miami, Florida, which he now calls home.

OBBA BABATUNDE

One of the wonderful things about this business is, no matter how long you've been in the business, you can always improve.

Obba Babatunde

It's very interesting for me. People ask me what do I like doing the most: acting, singing, or dancing. I started out in the business at a time when the images on television were taken from people like Sammy Davis, Jr., who did all these things: sing, dance and act, so I see them all as one art form.

I was born in Queens, New York, and majored in speech

and theatre in school. I did straight drama for a long time, until musicals became very lucrative for black performers in New York. That's how I really got involved in musicals.

I started out in the business as a musician and got my first professional job when I was only fourteen years old.

The training has been there and the honing of the craft. One of the wonderful things about this business is, no matter how long you've been in the business, you can always improve. And that's how I work at my craft.

For the role as a boxer in *Golden Boy*, I went into training in a weight-lifting program. I worked out in a professional boxing gym, and I tell you, I now have a great deal of respect and admiration for boxers and any athlete who is on a professional level. What they have to put themselves through in order to be able to maintain and withstand the punishment is quite exceptional. Doing *Golden Boy* was like a professional bout, so I'm real glad I did it. I originally did the show at "The Billie Holiday Theatre" in Brooklyn, then at the "Coconut Grove Playhouse" in Miami. Lewis Johnson, the choreographer, cast dancers who were trained in ballet, Jazz and Modern, and we all had to have that extra exceptional quality of being able to transfer those forms of dance into boxing moves. I warm up physically before a performance, working out with weights. I also do a vocal and dance warm-up.

Then, it's all technique. To sing and dance at the same time; knowing how to maintain your voice, how to sing a ballad after a big dance number, and pick a girl up in your arms at the same time. You have to learn the technique or you couldn't sustain and make it look easy.

Everybody tends to think that because you finally come into the public eye as a recognizable face or force in the industry, you're a new guy on the scene. No way. Generally speaking, the norm is that, that person has paid his dues.

I've always said I don't know where I'll be years from now.

I just know it will be in a better place, because I continue to work. And with everything having a level of combustion, you work to that level until it explodes into something even greater. That's the only thing I can hope to do.

OBBA BABATUNDE

Obba Babatunde, a Queens, New York, native, is an actor/singer/dancer/choreographer. A Tony nominee for his riveting portrayal of C. C. White in the Broadway smash *Dream Girls*, he also plays smooth Rusty Bennett on ABC's *All My Children* and has established himself as an artist with international appeal. In the lead performance in Hal Prince's award-winning Broadway musical *Grind*, he drew standing ovations and unanimous critical praise. As Joe Wellington in *Golden Boy*, he is utilizing his full stage repertoire, plus boxing skills, in this physically demanding role.

Believing he was destined for the spotlight, Obba began his professional quest towards stardom at age 14 as a fiery and gifted musician. He first appeared in *Timbuktu*, directed, costumed and choreographed by Geoffrey Holder and starring Eartha Kitt and Melba Moore. Following *Timbuktu* he appeared in *It's So Nice To Be Civilized, Guys and Dolls, Reggae* (with co-star Philip Michael Thomas), and *Treemonisha*, in which he played Zodzetrick. On the world tour and HBO special *Liza In Concert*, he co-starred with Liza Minnelli. With Nell Carter and Mikhail Baryshnikov, he was featured in the televised spectacular *Baryshnikov On Broadway*.

Commercials provide another creative outlet for Obba. He is a writer/producer/director as well as choreographer for club acts and has a production company of his own. In Nigeria his name translates into "King" (Obba) and "The spirit of the grandfather has returned in the child" (Babatunde).

BARRY BROWN

"I admire actors so much. I can't do what actors do."

Barry Brown

My dad was a music publisher. The firm published mostly theatre music, so I was brought up with it. I went to college to become a teacher, but went to work for Broadcast Music, Inc. (B.M.I.) and gravitated toward the theatre. I never wanted to be on stage. That really takes talent, but I think almost anyone can produce. If you want to produce a Broadway show, find a property that you like, raise the money, and bring it in. The trick is to keep it running, and making it a hit.

Most people think once a show is up and running, it runs itself. It just doesn't work that way. You have to advertise and keep the public informed, keep their interest up.

Let's use *Gypsy* as an example. I was sitting at home, flipping channels one night, and hit the *Dolly Parton Show*. There was Tyne Daly singing. I had an idea. I'd been thinking of doing *Gypsy*. I called Tyne's agent and asked if she'd play "Mama Rose" and he said yes. Just like that.

When I mentioned her to Arthur Laurents (who wrote the original play and would direct again), he said, "Well, she's got to come in and audition for Julie Styne and Steven Sondheim. She agreed and sang and they were "knocked out." Arthur said, "If she can sing 'Some People' she can sing anything." He also said, "Let's not audition in a rehearsal hall. We'll get a theatre." Tyne Daly auditioned on the stage of the Imperial Theatre. She's so wonderful. She doesn't think of herself as a star, but as a working actress.

Now, my job as Executive Producer began. I had a proven success with *Gypsy* so, it's being financed by private investors, whereas with *La Cage* I didn't, and had to run backers auditions, which we held in composer Jerry Herman's house.

After you raise the money, the director is the next step. He really is the Captain of the ship, although everyone does the casting together.

Very often, if I want a particular star, I can't get past the agent, who perhaps doesn't want his big film star to do a Broadway show, where there's no money, compared to a film. Sometimes, actors can't get past the casting director, when they'd love to do the role. Some agents and casting directors have been fired by their clients, under these circumstances.

During rehearsals, I stay in my office and work on advertising. I don't go to rehearsal unless I'm invited. I admire actors so much. I can't do what actors do. I can't take the rejection. Yes, I have had some flops. *Wally's Cafe* was one. It was a three-character comedy, and starred Jimmy Coco, Rita Moreno and Sally Struthers. Another flop was a big musical called *Platinum*, which starred Alexis Smith.

I'm looking forward to my next project which will be a revival of *Mr. Roberts* and will star Tom Selleck. I'm also looking for an original musical to star Angela Lansbury.

I must say I produce to pay the rent, and although there's no applause, I have a wonderful time.

BARRY BROWN

Barry Brown is on the Board of Governors of the League of American Theatres and Producers, and with his late partner, Fritz Holt, has been responsible for the London and American productions of *Gypsy* starring Angela Lansbury, Bette Midler's *Clams On The Half-Shell Revue*; the Tony Award-winning revival of *The Royal Family*; the original *Perfectly Frank*, later taped for TV starring Cloris Leachman; and Texaco Star Theatre Opening Night for NBC. They were responsible for the ground-breaking AIDS benefit *The Best Of The Best* at New York's Metropolitan Opera House in November, 1985. Mr. Brown is a recipient of the 1984 Tony Award as Producer of the musical *La Cage Aux Folles* and the 1990 Tony Award as producer of *Gypsy*. Currently he is Producing Artistic Director of the Long Beach, California, Civic Light Opera Company.

BUDDY CLARKE

"Push yourself. You never know what heights are within yourself till you try it."

Buddy Clarke

I was born and educated in New York City. I wanted to be a lawyer, but I graduated at fifteen, and they wouldn't let me into Law School then. So I went to the University of Alabama for an academic degree, and while there did my first radio show in Birmingham in 1929 as a singing soloist with the University of Alabama Glee Club. That kind of got me started in show business. I was blessed with a great ear for music, and had played the violin since I was four.

I worked in a country place one summer as a singer. A guy who was also on the bill knew a night club that needed a band in New York City. He asked if I could put a band together and I said, "Sure." That was the beginning of my "chutzpah." (Chutzpah, a Yiddish word that's become universal, meaning nerve; having the ability to do a lot of things you might not even be capable of, but having the nerve to try it.)

In those days, bands rehearsed at Nola Studios. There must have been forty bands rehearsing in forty different rooms. I went around, put my ear to each door and listened till I heard a band I liked, which I hired.

The night club was "Armando's," one of the swankiest in the city. There was "The Stork Club," "El Morocco" and "Armando's."

After two weeks the band gave me notice, cause they got $5.00 a man more to work The Arcadia Ballroom. I was heartbroken, but went back to Nola Studios and got an even better band that stayed with me all during my band career. I had been law-clerking during the day, but finally gave it up for full-time band leading, of which I only have fond memories.

I remember buying my way into "The Coconut Grove" in The Park Central Hotel in New York City. I bribed the agent with $1000 to put me in there. (More chutzpah.)

I remember saying sure I could conduct, when the famous "fan dancer" Sally Rand lost her conductor and I had to take over. That's when I discovered I had a photographic memory for music. I'd rehearse it, play one show and never need the music again.

I worked for five years in Montreal, Canada, in one of the top night clubs, conducting one-nighters for Milton Berle, Eddie Cantor, Danny Kaye and many, many big stars. I had a coast-to-coast radio show and was enjoying being a big fish in a little pond. During the war, I "enlisted" with my whole band in the Navy, and my law degree got me a commission.

Today I live and work in Miami, Florida. I "review" for radio and print, and I love it. I talked myself into being the movie critic for *Diario Las Americas,* the largest Spanish language daily in the southeast, and have been with them for seven years. I've interviewed some of the major film stars: George Burns, Raul Julia, James Wood, and on and on and on. To me that's a joy. I can write a one-minute pithy review for radio, or do it in 45 seconds if it's bad. I even got involved as a travel writer and get to go all over the world in exchange for my articles.

It's having faith in your own capabilities, with the desire to do anything to get there, that does it. I think everyone should finish schooling. The more education, with more degrees, the better you'll be able to cope with life.

Push yourself. You never know what heights are within yourself till you try it.

STEVE CONDOS

"Each teacher demonstrates his style, proving tap dancing is an art."

Steve Condos

I was raised in South Philadelphia, where my dad had a restaurant on 12th and South. It was a music and dancing neighborhood. Instead of playing games in the street, we danced. We danced our way to school, improvising and doing our own thing. I guess it was the equivalent of "street dancing" or the "break dancing" of today.

Across from my dad's restaurant was "The Standard

Theatre," where some of the greatest acts, like Louis Armstrong worked. They'd eat at our restaurant and do sessions there. We lived upstairs, and I'd sneak down and listen to them.

My older brother Frank danced in a minstrel show, then in a tap show and six months later was in a Broadway show. He took me to see the shows, and all I wanted to do was grow up and join him, which didn't quite work out that way. Frank and my brother Nick were working as "The Condos Brothers" when Frank left and I replaced him at "The Keith Theatre" in Brooklyn and then right into "The Palace" in New York.

My first job was in the "big time," but I was really bad in the beginning. Dancing in the street and on stage were two different things. But when I was surrounded by great talent like Jack Benny, pantomimist Jimmy Savo, James Barton and Patsy Kelly in Earl Carrol's "Vanities," I practiced and practiced, knowing I had to get good, to stay "up there" with them.

I came in at the end of Vaudeville and the beginning of the Night Club era. We played "The Chez Paree" in Chicago, "The Copa" and "Latin Quarter" in New York, and in California, "The Trocadero," on the same bill with Judy Garland, Fats Waller, and Tony Martin. Every act in that show got signed for films.

Daryl Zanuck put us in Sonja Henie's first film *Happy Landing*, then with Betty Grable in *Moon Over Miami* and *Pin-Up Girl*. Every time 20th Century Fox did a musical, they'd call us.

Nick and I broke up in 1945, when he married Martha Raye and managed her career. But, one of the greatest years of my life was when we played "The Palladium" in London, in 1940 . . . Nick couldn't care less. He had the most fantastic legs, but he hated to dance. He just wanted to make money. I was just the opposite. I loved it, but I wasn't business smart.

I continued as a single. In 1972, my career took another turn up, when I went into the Broadway show *Sugar!* It was my life for eight years. In 1988, Gregory Hines invited me to be in the film *Tap.* I had just had emergency surgery, and the studio couldn't get insurance for me. Gregory said, "No problem, I'll insure him!" He did and that's how I made the film.

On September 18, 1989, I danced in Carnegie Hall with nine "hoofers," including Gregory Hines and Jimmy Slyde, to a "sold-out" house. An electrifying night in my career.

Since 1985, I've been involved in Tap Festivals, enjoying the communicating and sharing with others, to keep tap alive, and to keep "passing it on." Each teacher demonstrates his style, proving tap dancing is an art.

What could be a happier ending than to be seventy-one years old and still be doing what you love!

* * * * *

Steve Condos died of a heart attack September 16, 1990, shortly after walking off stage at the Bienale de la Danse in Lyon, France.

JANE CONNELL

Jane Connell

"God gives us a certain amount of equipment, and I think you pray for the wisdom to know its limits as well as its extent."

Jane Connell

I was a character woman in the third grade, and that's what I've been ever since. It's been comedy most of the time. One comedy just seems to lead to another; although there's a lot of good drama in comedy. What is it they say? "There's always a tear behind every laugh." I've always enjoyed coming in and cleaning up with the jokes. Although in summer stock, years ago, in Sacramento, California, at

The Music Circus, I was in residence, and I got a chance to do everything. I even got to do LaLume in *Kismet* with a great deal of help from wigs and dresses, and things that were rather exotic.

But I think comedy comes from a way of looking at life. Kind of from a different angle. I grew up in a family that laughed a lot. If you've been in an environment where people don't take life too seriously and just see the funny side, it helps a lot.

I've never yearned to play Lady Macbeth. There are people born to do that. I believe in sticking to what you can do. God gives us a certain amount of equipment, and I think you pray for the wisdom to know its limits as well as its extent.

I've never studied or trained to be a singer, but I'm a great fan of real singers and musicians. I married one. I am musical, and since there's always been music in my house, I'm not afraid of it. I have an abandon that comes from ignorance.

When I was in rehearsal for *Mame* playing Gooch, and rehearsing "Gooch's Song," Jerry Herman said that "What Do I Do Now" refrain didn't sound right. He wanted me to do something outrageous with it, so at the end I hit a B-flat, which I could never do today. Now every poor kid who plays Gooch has to hit that note, and it was just a whim.

No matter what we do though, I think there's a sixth sense that we use to communicate. That's the trick. The audience must feel a part of the show. They really are a participant, whether it's serious drama or high comedy. They're like a member of the cast, and every night is a different show, because the audience is different every night.

In order to sustain eight performances a week, I gear my life around it. I advise sleeping late, eating well and making your portrayal on stage as honest as is humanly possible.

JANE CONNELL

Jane Connell was Angela Lansbury's original Agnes Gooch in *Mame* and returned to Broadway for the 1983 revival after having made the film with Lucille Ball. Her other Broadway shows include *New Faces of '56*, *Dear World*, and *Me And My Girl*, for which she received a 1987 Tony nomination. Julius Monk presented her in *Cabaret* and Ben Bagley's *Shoestring '55* provided the first of her many Off-Broadway performances, which include Mrs. Peachum in the Theatre de Lys' *The Threepenny Opera*; Mrs. Hardcastle and Mrs. Malaprop at the Roundabout; Lady Wishfort at the Long Wharf; and Miss Prism at The Mark Taper in Los Angeles. Queen Victoria on TV's *Bewitched*; Princess Winifred in *Once Upon A Mattress* at London's Adelphi Theatre; Miss Hannigan in the national company of *Annie*; and Dorothy Parker in the one-woman show *The Singular Dorothy Parker* at New York City's Actor's Playhouse are among her favorite roles. Her most recent Broadway appearance was in *Lend Me A Tenor*.

CAROLE COOK

"Anybody has a shot at this business. Some just have to work harder."

Carole Cook

I was born in a small town, Abilene, Texas. My mom was sort of a rural Auntie Mame. She took me to see the "Lunts" and people of that era, but she certainly didn't know anything about show business.

I remember reading in a movie magazine that Rosalind Russell weighed 129 pounds, and I thought, isn't that wonderful, so do I. The fact that I was only nine years old didn't bother me at all.

I was so damn unattractive, but no one ever told me. In fact, pregnant women wouldn't look at me on the street for fear it would mark their unborn child.

Show business was a fantasy for me. I can't remember ever not wanting to be an actress. It's like a "calling."

I think I was born funny. I think you have to be, and that sort of a natural talent is necessary. As an actress, you can learn pretty good timing, and you can improve it as you become professional. But extraordinary timing can't be taught.

I studied drama under Paul Baker at Baylor University in Texas and got my "Masters" in Greek Drama.

I went to New York and on my first professional audition I got the part of Mrs. Peachum in *The Threepenny Opera* and played it for a year.

While touring in stock, Lucille Ball heard of me and brought me to Hollywood and put me under contract at Desilu. Lucy played a very big part in my early career and was matron of honor at my wedding.

I advise newcomers to study and work in any show anywhere. Get a job waiting tables, anything to keep things comfortable until a paying job comes along.

Anybody has a shot at this business. Some just have to work harder.

CAROLE COOK

Carole Cook created the role of Maggie Jones in the New York, Los Angeles and Tokyo companies of the Tony Award winning musical *42nd Street.* This followed her Broadway appearance opposite Mia Farrow and Anthony Perkins in Bernard Slade's *Romantic Comedy.* She was the first actress following Carol Channing to play Dolly Levi in an 18-month Australia-New Zealand tour of *Hello Dolly!* Most recently she starred as Mame at the Burt Reynolds Jupiter Theatre. *Steel Magnolias* marks her third collaboration with Barbara Rush. They first starred together in the Los Angeles and National companies of Oliver Hailey's *Father's Day,* which won Ms. Cook a Los Angeles Drama Critic's nomination for her portrayal of the bitter and brittle divorcee, Louise. She later went on to star in the Australian production.

She worked with Ms. Rush again in George Furth's *The Supporting Cast* for which she won a Best Actress Drama-Logue Award. She starred in Los Angeles and Dallas in Jack Heifner's *Patio/Porch* for which she was awarded the Drama-Logue and Robby Best Actress Awards. Some of her other stage roles include Amanda in *Private Lives,* Regina in *The Little Foxes,* the title roles in *Madwoman Of Chaillot, Auntie Mame, The Matchmaker,* and *The Bald Soprano,* and a tour of her one-woman show, *Dress Up.*

Her feature films include *The Incredible Mr. Limpet, Palm Springs Weekend, The Gauntlet, American Gigolo, Grandview U.S.A., Summer Lovers,* and *Sixteen Candles.* Television audiences have seen her in the recurring roles of Donna LaMar in *Cagney & Lacey* and Cora in *Dynasty.* She was a regular on the *Merv Griffin Show* and has frequently guest-starred on shows such as *Magnum, P.I., Hart to Hart, The Love Boat, Knight Rider,* and *Murder She Wrote.*

She is married to actor-director Tom Troupe, who besides playing her on-stage ex-husband in *Father's Day,* also directed her in the American and Australian productions, as well as *The Supporting Cast, Dress Up,* and *Patio/Porch.* They co-starred in the Dallas Theatre Center's production of *The Lion In Winter.*

CONSTANCE CUMMINGS

"It's surprising what you find in your own guts that you can bring out."

Constance Cummings

I began by performing in choruses on Broadway, followed by a move to Hollywood where I made a few films. I consider myself lucky. I never had to struggle.

I moved to England to do a film and married Benn Levy, who eventually directed many of my performances, including *Sour Grapes*, my first London success.

My happiest experience on the stage was *Long Days Journey Into Night* in which I performed with Laurence Olivier. The play was a huge success at the National Theatre. We had a good cast, and we all worked so well together.

We only had a few hours each day to rehearse, as the two actors who played the sons were performing in another production as well at The National Theatre. We rehearsed for a few months, and we became integrated as a family. We would sit together and talk . . . reading the play. We became so immersed in our characters that on opening night, when we saw the audience for the first time, we were shocked and slightly taken aback to see people looking into our "family."

In 1940, I did Sartre's *No Exit* in London. Playing this character, who was cast into Hell, was a turning point in my development as an actor. First, I didn't think I could play the role. The character was a vicious, wicked, harsh woman, and I'd never played anybody like that before. The director kept trying to convince me that I could play the part. I finally tried for the role, and it opened a lot of doors for me.

After that, it was easier to play Martha in *Who's Afraid Of Virginia Woolf?* years later in London.

Because of *No Exit*, I can't think of anything that I wouldn't try to play.

As a result of everything I've learned in my many, many years in this business, I can only advise young actors, starting out, to go ahead and have a go at it; have a try. It's surprising what you find in your own guts that you can bring out. The essence of being an actor is that you sympathize with all the possibilities of the human character, all the smart people, dumb people, good people, bad people, beautiful people, ugly people. You have all of these people in you.

CONSTANCE CUMMINGS

Constance Cummings has established a rich and extensive career on both stage and screen. A Tony Award recipient for Best Actress for her performance in Arthur Kopit's *Wings* on Broadway, Ms. Cummings also appeared in the successful Broadway production of *Accent Of Youth*.

In England, she appeared at the prestigious Old Vic, Albert Hall and Festival Hall. At the Albert Hall, she narrated Prokofiev's *Peter And The Wolf* and was the first in England to play Joan in the Claudel-Honnegger oratorio, *St. Joan At The Stake*. In England's National Theatre, Ms. Cummings played Volumnia in *Coriolanus*, Leda in *Amphytryon*, Mary Tyrone in *Long Days Journey Into Night*, and Madame Ranevsky in *The Cherry Orchard*. At the Mermaid Theatre, she played in A. R. Gurney's *Children*.

Her other stage credits include: *Taming Of The Shrew, Madame Bovary, Lysistrata*, Huxley's *The Genius And The Goddess, Who's Afraid Of Virginia Woolf?* and Noel Coward's *Fallen Angels*. Ms. Cummings's numerous films include *Blithe Spirit* and *The Battle Of The Sexes*. Among her radio and television credits, she has played *St. Joan, Hedda Gabler*, Shakespeare's *Cleopatra* and *Craig's Wife*. In addition, she has appeared in the PBS Production of *Wings* in Los Angeles.

PHYLLIS DILLER

"When it looks 'easy,' you're looking at art!"

Phyllis Diller

I was a "late bloomer!" I started my career when I was 37. At that time I was a housewife, a mother of five children, and I worked as a publicist at radio station KSFO in San Francisco. My husband, then, Sherwood Diller, urged me on to prepare a night club act. I did and was booked into San Francisco's "Purple Onion." I slithered around the piano, lampooned current celebrities, made fun of high fashion and life in general. I was booked for two weeks and stayed for 89.

If you want to be a comic, find out if you have what it takes to be funny. It's a long road from the living room to the night clubs. Can you take the rejection? You have to be very well adjusted, or it can kill you. Not everyone can do it. You can still be a famous actor, but not necessarily in comedy.

Can you handle an audience? I've learned to never ask a question of the audience; that invites heckling. You mustn't break the screen, or they'll feel they can talk, too. You must be the leader, so they'll hush and listen. You have a role to play, and they have a role to play. Stay in charge. If you let them speak to you, they'll ruin your timing. I edit my words so I can deliver as many as twelve punch lines a minute.

When I started, I toured, polishing my act. I played "The Blue Angel" in New York and appeared on the *Jack Parr Show*. From that point, my career rocketed.

A great many people ask me how to get into show business, simply because I'm in it. Most people erroneously think it's "who you know, not what you know!" That couldn't be further from the truth. It is "what you know."

Novices always think you start out with an agent, a manager and a press agent. So wrong. Supposing you start on some kind of show biz job at scale. You're making $150.00 a week.

That gives your agent $15.00 a week. What kind of a crummy agent could live on $15.00 a week? Or what agency in America would bother with an act where the paper work costs more than the income?

With a scale act there is nothing to manage. So you don't need a manager.

An agency doesn't make a cent on an act till the act is making $1500 a week.

Now . . . so much for the wrong thinking about how to get into show biz. You see, the wrong thinking is all based on fear, on wanting lots of help, wanting somebody else to do all the work. People who think show biz is all glamour sometimes think there is nothing to it, just walk out and be gorgeous, walk out and sing, or dance, or talk.

Into all branches of show business go years of work, experience or training, or all three. When it looks "easy," you're looking at art!

To get into show biz, you start right where you are. You act, or sing, or whatever it is you want to do. You offer to do it for nothing, or maybe later making a little money from your appearances after people have seen you.

There are those who think you have to go to Hollywood or New York to get into the business. I say . . . a trip around the world starts with the first step, and the first step can only be taken in one spot, where you're standing now.

Once you're working, taste is as important as talent. A lot of people who are loaded with talent have no taste. They can't possibly ever make it.

Believing in yourself completely is imperative. Every doubt you have weakens you. You have to be able to face humiliating failure. You have to have great stamina, and excellent health.

People have a completely mistaken idea about "breaks." There is no such thing as "breaks." If you're looking for "breaks," you've got your eye on the wrong thing.

Many people turn down opportunities because they are usually disguised as "hard work." You'd be amazed the people who will not go out on a limb, or progress, or change, and hurt a little for awhile, to expand their powers.

Most are prone to take the easy way, the comfy way. If you're not hurting a little, you're not growing.

Back when I first got into the business and I used to go to auditions, I set up one of my first rules. Perform, entertain. Don't "show off."

I would see these acts who tried to show how talented

they were. They did everything, and nothing. They were so busy showing off they forgot to entertain. They were disgusting. You disliked them.

An entertainer should never give up on stage. No matter how badly things are going, you keep right on as if everything was all right.

A performer who consistently blames "the audience" will never make it. There is no such thing as a bad audience, only a bad performance.

After all, they're there. They paid to see you. You're supposed to be the leader and take them where you please. You should not be affected by them; they should be affected by you. If they aren't, you're not strong enough to be up there in the white hot lights.

Being well received by a small community or by friends is far different than being a pro and being well received by strangers, or the public.

When Steve Allen is asked how you go about becoming a comic, he says: "If by the time you're twelve years old, you aren't a comic, don't give it another thought."

My career started with poverty. Poverty is a wonderful motivator. Now I'm 73 years old, and it's not just the plastic surgery that keeps me pretty; it's happiness. I love everything I'm doing.

PHYLLIS DILLER

Born Phyllis Driver in Lima, Ohio, on July 17, 1917, Phyllis Diller was an only child of older parents. She graduated from Central High School in 1935 and studied at Sherwood Music Conservatory in Chicago for three years. Music studies continued at Bluffton College in Bluffton, Ohio, where she met her first husband, Sherwood Diller.

In the course of her career, Miss Diller has won numerous awards in recognition of her talent, her patriotic and her philanthropic activities. She is a former honorary mayor of Brentwood, California, and received a Ph.D. ("Is that an abbreviation of Phyllis Diller?") degree in Humane Letters from National Christian University in Dallas and a Doctorate from Kent State. Other honors are the Golden Apple from the Hollywood Women's Press Club as most cooperative actress, the USO Liberty Bell Award, for demonstrating in 1981; she received the AMC Cancer Institute Humanitarian Award; and was inducted into Ohio's Women's Hall of Fame for her contribution as entertainer, author and actress. She was featured on Ralph Edwards *This is Your Life* in 1971.

Her movie credits include: *Splendor in the Grass; The Fat Spy; Boy, Did I Get A Wrong Number; Eight On The Lamb; Mad Monster Party; Did You Hear The One About The Traveling Saleslady?; Private Navy of Sgt. O'Farrel; The Adding Machine; The Sunshine Boys; A Pleasure Doing Business*; and *Motel.*

NANETTE FABRAY

"Technique should be in your body, in your genes almost, by the time you get to do a show."

Nanette Fabray

I started when I was three, in a little tap school in Los Angeles. I won the local talent contest. The first prize was a week's engagement at The Paramount Theater in Los Angeles. Later on, I did some extra work in movies until I won a scholarship to The Max Reinhardt School. His school was the best. John Houston taught us motion picture camera technique; a Russian teacher taught us ballet; an Olympic champion fencer taught us fencing. Max Reinhardt felt if you want to be in the theater, you must know everything. We had to write a play and put it on. We learned costume design and scenic design. He really made us learn our trade in that school.

Often I'll go to a college and talk to the senior drama class and ask, "What do you know about getting out of a chair, or coming through the door, or walking down a flight of stairs, or body language?" Usually I get blank stares, so I say, "What have you been studying for four years?" Now, I can see the teacher getting angry with me. They'll answer, "Well, we've been studying art and drama and the meaning of the play." Would a concert violinist think of going to Carnegie Hall before learning scales?

What Max Reinhardt taught is still relevant today, and I'm still using the technique. Technique should be in your body, in your genes almost, by the time you get to do a show.

I'll never forget the time I was on tour with a play, in Louisville at The Ford Theatre. Nobody told me the stage was "raked" (slanted). I made my entrance way upstage in a big 72-pound hoop skirt, and it carried me right onto the drums in the orchestra pit. That was learning the meaning of upstage and downstage the hard way. The Ford was a very old theater, and in the "olden days" the stages were "raked" and the audience was flat. That was also a lesson for me: never try anything without a rehearsal.

I've danced all my life and never lost it, because I kept doing it. I danced with Fred Astaire in the movie *Bandwagon*. He made it look so easy, 'cause every dance we did, we rehearsed for at least a month. Fortunately, dance was as much a part of me as walking was, and still is. That's why I can never think of retiring. I can understand people retiring who have worked hard at a job they don't like, but if you like what you do, why stop? I can't believe I get paid.

(Don't tell the producers I said that.)

NANETTE FABRAY

Nanette Fabray recently starred in her own one-woman show *Yes, Yes, Nanette*, produced by Danny Daniels. She has been honored many times by her peers and by the public. She received two Donaldson Awards for her work in the hit Broadway musical *High Button Shoes* and a Tony Award for *Love Life*. Other Broadway shows include *By Jupiter, Make A Wish, Bloomer Girl, Mr. President*, and *No Hard Feelings*. Her movies include *The Bandwagon, That's Entertainment II* and others.

She won three Emmy Awards for her comedic work with Sid Caesar in the hit TV show *Caesar's Hour*, and she completed six years as Katherine Romano in the hit TV show *One Day At A Time*. In 1986 the Screen Actors Guild gave her their highest honor — the Humanitarian Award.

Radio and TV editors selected her as American Woman of the Year. She has been the Honorary Mayor of her home town, Pacific Palisades, and received the Fashion Academy Award as one of the ten best-dressed women in America.

Miss Fabray has been in the forefront of the fight for the rights of all handicapped people. She is a Board Member of the President's Committee on Employment of the Handicapped, a Trustee of the House Ear Institute, a Board Member of both the National Captioning Institute and the Better Hearing Institute in Washington, D. C. President Reagan re-appointed her to the National Council on the Handicapped. This year, Congress appointed her to the Commission on Education of the Deaf.

For these and similar efforts, she has received the President's distinguished service award, The Eleanor Roosevelt

Humanitarian Award, the California Museum of Science and Industry Woman of the Year Award, three honorary Doctorates and numerous other similar honors. She and Helen Keller are the only women to receive the public service award, American Academy of Otolaryngology. She says her finest achievement is her son Jamie MacDougall, who graduated from USC Medical School in 1984.

JOSE FERRER

"The highest accolade that could be paid me is to have anyone think he could do what I have spent over fifty years of my life learning to do."

Jose Ferrer

I had no training whatsoever. I learned because I was fortunate to work with some very great directors. I remember five in particular who completely shaped my thinking: Joshua Logan, Guthrie McLintic, George Abbott, Howard Lindsay and Jed Harris. I learned something from each of them. From McLintic, I felt a great liberation of emotion. I adored him. I did four plays for him and would get so moved in rehearsal watching a scene, or reading a scene, or interpreting a scene, that I felt free to do anything, because he was so free. He'd say, "The theatre must be some place where you can expose yourself naked; and if the play demands a total freedom of emotional expression, don't be ashamed, don't be inhibited. An art form is not a place to be careful."

From George Abbott, I learned the mechanics of efficiency on stage. From Josh Logan I learned a great deal on how a play is written, how a play is constructed, so that as an actor I learned to be an efficient piece of machinery.

From Howard Lindsay, I learned general things. He was my first employer on Broadway, and I never stopped watching him wander around the set and talk to the actors.

I saved Jed Harris for last, because he was the greatest influence of them all. From Jed I learned the value of understatement. I think he was the most "elegant" director I ever worked for. His production of *Our Town* was a model of achieving enormous emotional results.

I like to think, in the work that permits it, both as a director and as an actor, that I would like the audience to feel that anyone could do it, that the artist is doing nothing at all. The highest accolade that could be paid me is to have anyone think he could do what I have spent over fifty years of my life learning to do. From Jed, I learned that you must be proud to appear to be doing nothing and to accomplish as much as God has given you the tools to accomplish.

Mostly, I was lucky. People liked me. When I walked on stage, I was always interesting. It's something God gives you, so you can't take credit for it. People would say, "I want him" — although I occasionally did get fired.

I rehearsed for three days in *Stage Door* with Margaret Sullavan. She had asked for me when they were looking for one particular character. But Edna Ferber said, "I don't like him," and out I went. But everyone's been fired.

When I was young, I didn't know how to rehearse. I had so many questions, and since I didn't have any formal training, I went into every rehearsal with a million question marks in front of me. The directors who cared about me, or who had faith in me, or who had no choice but to use me, helped to steer me. Then when I got in front of an audience, something happened. I suddenly had a reason to act.

I imitated my heroes, Alfred Lunt, Paul Muni, John Barrymore, and Laurence Olivier. Olivier wasn't much older than I was in time, but he was older professionally. He started acting at a much younger age. I joined Actors Equity when I was twenty-three. A late starter.

I also went to every show I could. I'd go to the box office and say, "I'm a young Equity actor," and ask if I could stand. They'd say, "Sure, go ahead." I made a point to see flops. I wanted to see why plays failed. When I'd see a performance I liked, I'd see it over and over again. I saw *Victoria Regina* with Helen Hayes four times. I saw Maurice Evans in *Richard II* — six times. I stood there and tried to learn. I'd go home and stand in front of a mirror and try to imitate, to do what they did.

I had read an interview with Basil Rathbone, before I ever did a film, in which he said, "In film acting, all you have to do is think." That really stuck in my mind and also helped me.

The bottom line is: Wear your heart on your sleeve, have a lot of courage, do not be deterred by pain, anguish, self-doubt and rejection. Just Do It!!!

JOSE FERRER

Jose Ferrer is regarded as one of the most versatile talents in the entertainment world, having established a reputation as a forceful actor and astute director of both stage and screen. He has won numerous Tony and Oscar Awards as well as three Critics Circle Awards. Audiences world-wide remember his award-winning performance as Cyrano de Bergerac on Broadway in 1946. His impressive list of Broadway credits includes *The Silver Whistle*, Iago in *Othello*, and directing and starring in *Twentieth Century* with Gloria Swanson. Mr. Ferrer won three Critics Circle Awards and two Tony Awards for his direction and performance in *The Shrike* in addition to starring in *The Girl Who Came To Supper* and *Man of La Mancha*.

His film credits include an Academy Award-winning performance in *Cyrano De Bergerac* and an Oscar nomination for his portrayal of the Dauphin in *Joan Of Arc*, his first motion picture performance. Nominated for a third Oscar for his performance as Toulouse Lautrec in *Moulin Rouge*, Mr. Ferrer has also appeared in *Miss Sadie Thompson, The Caine Mutiny, Deep in My Heart, Lawrence of Arabia, The Shrike, Ship of Fools*, and *Nine Hours to Rama*. His recent films include *A Midsummer Night's Sex Comedy* and *Dune*. On television Ferrer has narrated documentaries, starred in two productions of *Cyrano De Bergerac* and appeared in *Evita, The Young Harry Houdini*, and *The Dream Merchants*, to name just a few productions.

ESTELLE GETTY

"Trust the director, trust the material and play the truth."

Estelle Getty

I tried to be a "stand-up" comedienne, but it was at the wrong time. When I was young, people hated to see women try to be funny. They thought it was vulgar. I had very good material, and I honestly think I would have been successful if I was doing it at a time when it was more acceptable.

I think I was born funny. I don't think it's something you can learn. My father was a very funny man. I think I inherited his humor.

When I failed at stand-up comedy, I went right to theatre and felt at home. I got involved in a "professional" community theatre in Queens, New York. We were all professional actors who moved to the suburbs to raise our kids; to do all the things Mommys and Daddys do and still be actors. We trained there, too. We had workshops and "imported" teachers from "the city."

I played Mrs. Beckoff in *Torch Song Trilogy* for four years with great joy. I did it first at "La Mama," then off-off Broadway, off-Broadway, on-Broadway and on tour. I never tired of it 'cause it's such a good play.

Most of the roles I've done have been magnificently written. That's because I've played a lot of mothers. No matter how good or bad a playwright is, his depiction of the mother, on stage, or in a movie, is always going to be the best. I don't know why that is, but it is. There'll be endless roles for me, since everyone had a mother.

After *Torch Song Trilogy*, I thought I'd never get anything but roles like Mrs. Beckoff. But, when I hit California, all kinds of roles were offered to me.

When I saw the description of Sophia for *Golden Girls*, I thought, it's not for me. I pictured her European looking, rotund, wearing her slick black hair in a bun. I discussed this with my friend Joel Kimmel, a comedy writer. He advised me to do what I do well; 'cause, "If they like you, they'll change the character. If you bring in a reading that's dynamic, original and good, they'll make the adjustment," he said. It took five auditions, and an old lady's thrift shop outfit, to prove I could do it.

I knew *Golden Girls* was going to be a hit, but I had no idea it would be the Mega-hit that it is.

Although "acting is acting," the transition to TV has been very difficult for me. It's hard to be funny on cue, and do it over and over again.

I remember when I first started, I was reacting to everything, like when I was on stage. One of the cameramen said to me, "You're great. You even act when the camera isn't on you." I've learned acting for TV "on the job" — how to bring things "down;" to bring it into focus; to be angry without raising the voice. It's a matter of intensity.

My credo for acting, in general, has always been, less is more. Trust the material, trust the director, and play the truth. Then you won't have to do anything more. I simply believe in the person I'm playing and play the part of her that loves. Sophia can be a cantankerous old lady, but I think she's a very loving and caring person.

What I've learned about this business is there are no rules. There are two areas in the world that I know that you make no judgments. One is how to become a success in this business and how long it will take. The other is how to raise the kids that you want.

You think if you work hard and you do all the right things, and you do your homework and learn your craft, you're going to become a success. Not necessarily so. There are people who haven't done that and become successful!

The only way to stay alive in this business is to want it more than anything else and to let nothing discourage you.

I think people starting out today should start in theatre, as I did. That's where the craft is born. If you do theatre, you can do anything else. The reverse is not necessarily true.

Opportunities today are more limited because there are so many more talented actors than there used to be, because so many are freer to make the choice. The competition is so incredible.

My success with *Golden Girls* got me the invitation to write a book. It's a series of observations; my feelings and reactions.

I initially wanted to call it *I'm Absolutely Sure About This,*

I Think! But, *If I Knew Then What I Know Now, So What,* won out.

Although I love *Golden Girls* and plan to stay with it as long as I can, it's really my last go-round. I don't think I'll ever find anything as good again.

ESTELLE GETTY

Estelle Getty was born and raised in New York City, and was trained for the stage by The Herbert Berghof Studios, Gerard Russak and Irene Dailey.

Her portrayal of Mrs. Beckoff in *Torch Song Trilogy* won her the first ever Helen Hayes Award as best supporting performer.

Her other theatre credits include: *The Divorce of Judy Jane, Table Settings, I'm Not Jewish and I Don't Know Why I'm Screaming*, and Sidney Morris' *A Gallery Of Characters.*

On tour and in regional theatres: *Come Blow Your Horn, Last Of The Red Hot Lovers, Lovers And Other Strangers, 6 Rooms River Vu, The Importance Of Being Earnest, Blithe Spirit, Separate Tables, A Visit To A Small Planet*, and *Call Me By My Rightful Name.*

Estelle has received four Emmy nominations and one Emmy Award, a Golden Globe Award, and a Golden Apple for her portrayal of Sophia on *The Golden Girls.*

Other TV and film credits include: *No Man's Land* with Stella Stevens, *Mask*, as Cher's mother, *Copacabana* as Barry Manilow's mother, as well as *Fantasy Island, Cagney and Lacey, The Bob Newhart Show, Mannequin, Tootsie* and *Hotel* with Elizabeth Taylor.

Miss Getty is a National Spokesperson for Purina Pets, for Older People and is active in raising funds for AIDS and for the homeless.

JACK GILFORD

"I was never an actor who wanted to play Shakespeare. My goal was to be as funny as I could."

Jack Gilford

In the 30's, during the depression, there were talent nights in New York, organized by agents. The show would consist of five acts, a Master of Ceremonies and a pianist. I did "mimicry," of George Jessel, Laurel and Hardy, and Rudy Vallee among others. From this I just barely made a living. I remember when I was only five or six years old, I could imitate the walk of people, and having gotten a few laughs, I was hooked.

I didn't study because I didn't know where or what school to latch on to. I learned about acting in 1955 playing in *The Diary of Anne Frank* for two years. It was a very serious role. Garson Kanin took a chance and gave me the part.

It was also Garson Kanin who cast me in *Die Fledermaus*, which he directed. Danny Kaye was supposed to do it; but fortunately for me, he was too busy. The role was the drunken jailer. My entrance was to fall down a flight of fifteen steps. I played it very burlesque. Although I never played Burlesque Houses, like so many comedians, I did have the opportunity to do burlesque skits at the resort "Green Mansions." When we ran out of material, we'd fill in with burlesque skits.

I was never an actor who wanted to play Shakespeare. My goal was to be as funny as I could. I'm often remembered for the "Crackerjack" commercial I did that ran for eleven years. That was funny. It won Clio's and The Cannes Festival Award.

I have originated roles in *Cabaret, A Funny Thing Happened On The Way To The Forum, No, No, Nanette* and *The World of Sholem Aleichem*. I often get letters from young people in school telling me they're playing my role and could I give them some tips.

Well, when I sing, I think if I do something distracting with my hands or my face, maybe they won't listen so sharply. I have what I call a living room voice. Simply, actors are the most frightened, fearful, unsure, insecure people in the world. But, we're also very, very brave just to do it!

* * * * *

Jack Gilford died of cancer on June 4, 1990.

JACK GILFORD

Jack Gilford began his career as a vaudeville comedian. He appeared in the *Milton Berle Revue* from 1935–1939, made his Broadway debut in *Meet The People* in 1940, and his film debut in *Hey Rookie*.

Other films include: *Main Street To Broadway, A Funny Thing Happened On The Way To The Forum, Enter Laughing, Who's Minding The Mint?, The Incident, Catch 22, Save The Tiger, Harvey and Walter Go To New York, Cocoon*, and *Cocoon II*.

TV: *Happy, Hostage Flight, Arrow Show, Gary Moore Show, Milton Berle Show, Jack Carson Show, Frank Sinatra Show, The World of Sholem Aleichem, Cowboy and The Tiger, Once Upon A Mattress, Wholly Moses, Cheaper to Keep Her, Caveman, The Very Special Jack Gilford Special*, and *Apple Pie*.

Theatre: Frosch in *Die Fledermaus*, Bontche Schweig in *The World of Sholem Aleichem, Passion Of Gross, Once Over Lightly, Diary of Ann Frank, Romanoff and Juliet, Drink To Me Only, Once Upon A Mattress, The Tenth Man, The Policeman, Cabaret, Three Men On A Horse, A Funny Thing Happened On The Way To The Forum, No, No, Nanette, The Sunshine Boys, Sly Fox*, and *The Supporting Cast*.

DAN GOGGIN

"I think recognizing the sense of humor most nuns and priests have, helped me make the show a success."

Dan Goggin

We started *Nunsense* actually as a joke, with greeting cards. Marilyn Farina, who is very funny, was the main character in the greeting card; so we decided to send her to the card stores, as the Mother Superior, to do this little act, to hype the sale of the cards. She was so funny, we began to build a cabaret show around it.

We did the cabaret show at "The Duplex" in New York. It

was such a big success that it ran for 38 weeks. I was told to enlarge it into a musical comedy.

We put it on first as a workshop. Once again, we were very successful. We had a chance to move it into "The Cherry Lane Theatre," but we would have had to raise $150,000 in three weeks. Fortunately, a friend came in and saw the show and gave us $25,000 and that started the ball rolling. We called friends, who didn't have the money, but offered them a share if they could bring in some friends. Before we knew it, we had the money. It opened at "The Cherry Lane Theatre" on December 12, 1985, and has been running ever since. Now it's at The Fairbanks Theatre on 42 Street, "Theatre Row" in New York.

It's interesting how things happened to get *Nunsense* on. We've said many times that not "knowing the ropes" actually helped a great deal, because we didn't know there were things you couldn't achieve; and somehow magically, they happened.

I put *Nunsense* together and I felt I could direct it, because the characters were based on people I really knew. All my young life, I was a Seminary student. First in Catholic School, then the Seminary. We based the characters on the very nuns who taught me. Before writing, I had been a singer and I toured in a folk act, where we did a lot of satirical material. That gave me pretty good training in comedy timing.

Wisely, I steered clear of religious beliefs in the show. The humor comes from nuns trying to put on this entertainment, and I let the lyrics tell the story.

We've had seven companies running simultaneously, and every company is different. To date, Kaye Ballard, Dody Goodman, Marcia Lewis, Alice Ghostly, Jaye P. Morgan, Phyllis Diller, Peggy Cass, and Pat Carroll have performed as our nuns, and our best shows have been when we have nuns and priests in the audience.

I came to New York as an aspiring singer, but what opened "doors" for me was the show *Legend.* I wrote the score and it starred Elizabeth Ashley and F. Murray Abraham. Fortunately, we did an album. Although, the show didn't make it, the album gave me recognition.

I think recognizing the sense of humor most nuns and priests have, helped me make the show a success. Maybe my sense of humor got me where I am today. I've completed the writing of the screenplay, so maybe I can end by saying, "Be sure to see the film!"

DAN GOGGIN

Dan Goggin came to New York from Alma, Michigan, in 1963, as an aspiring singer. He landed a part on Broadway in John Osborne's *Luther,* then toured for five years in the satirical folk singing duo, The Saxons. He then turned his talents to writing and directing. He wrote the score for the off-Broadway musical *Hark*; the Broadway production *Legend,* starring Elizabeth Ashley and F. Murray Abraham; *Seven,* starring Jane White; and two revues, *Because We're Decadent* and *Something For Everybody's Mother.* Goggin has just completed writing a new musical, *A One-Way Ticket To Broadway,* and is currently completing the screenplay for a feature film of *Nunsense.*

Goggin's original cabaret review, *The Nunsense Story,* played for 38 weeks at the Duplex in Manhattan. He then developed the book musical *Nunsense* which was tried as a workshop production in the summer of 1985 at the Baldwin Theatre. It opened on December 12, 1985, off-Broadway at "The Cherry Lane Theatre," then moved in February, 1986, to the Sheridan Square Playhouse, Circle Rep Theatre, garnering critical acclaim and ever-increasing audiences. It has been playing at the Douglas Fairbanks Theatre off-Broadway since the fall of 1986. There have been some 55 companies of *Nunsense* world-wide, including those currently in New York; Boston; Philadelphia; Chicago; San Francisco; Orlando; Rochester and Cohoes, New York; Montreal and Edmonton, Ontario, Canada; Dublin, Ireland; Australia; Rio de Janerio, Brazil; Spain; Holland and Japan.

DODY GOODMAN

"It's never just one person who believes in you and encourages you. You're like a ball. You have to hit it this way and that way until you rise higher."

Dody Goodman

I wanted very much to be a "Ballerina." I started dancing school when I was eight years old in Columbus, Ohio, and went every day. When I graduated from high school, I thought if I'm going to make this my career, I'll have to go someplace where they hire dancers. Columbus, Ohio, did not have a ballet company.

I went to New York with another girl from my dancing school and her brother. He was a singer and had a lot of experience in New York. He kind of looked after us, and showed us the ropes. I got a job in the Corps de Ballet with the Opera, and then with Radio City Music Hall Ballet Corps.

I was cast in the musical *Wonderful Town* starring Rosalind Russell and Edie Adams. I was in the chorus, but for the first time I was given a part with two small scenes. George Abbott singled me out for that. It was the first time I opened my mouth, on stage. When *Wonderful Town* closed on Broadway, we went to Dallas, Texas, with Imogene Coca starring. She really encouraged me. But I find it's never just one person who believes in you and encourages you. A stage manager told me once not to depend on just one person to help you along. Remember you're like a ball. You have to hit it this way and that way until you rise higher.

I had a terrible time letting people know I could do other things besides dance. I remember the first show I got in as a comedienne. It was Ben Bagley's *Shoestring Revue*. Also in the cast were Chita Rivera, Bea Arthur and Artie Johnson.

It was sort of a beginning for all of us in comedy. I didn't even want to audition for the show. Although I had prepared some comedy material, I felt I wasn't ready. But a friend of mine, Michael Stewart (who later wrote the book for *Hello Dolly* and *42nd Street*), made an appointment for me and insisted I keep it. I did and I was chosen.

Today, people can't believe I was a serious ballet dancer. Yet, when I first started, people said, "You should do comedy." When I asked, "How do you do comedy?" they told me to be myself. Well, how do you do that?

You don't. The answer is, you have to develop a character. I think I did and that's what made me successful.

DODY GOODMAN

Dody Goodman, star of stage, film and television, began her career as a dancer before gaining a reputation as an extraordinary comedienne. She danced in such Broadway musicals as *High Button Shoes, Call Me Madam, Miss Liberty* and *Wonderful Town*. It was during *Wonderful Town* that actress Imogene Coca convinced her to put her dancing shoes aside and concentrate on comedy as a career. Ms. Goodman's comedic style has entertained audiences in such Broadway productions as *Period Of Adjustment; My Daughter, Your Son; Rainy Day In Newark,* and the revival of *The Front Page*. Her last stage performance was in *Ah, Wilderness!* for which she received a Drama Desk Award nomination.

To television audiences, Dody was the beloved "Resident Zany" on Jack Parr's *Tonight Show*. She is perhaps best known for her role of Martha Shumway on the popular series *Mary Hartman, Mary Hartman* and later, on *Forever Fernwood* on which she appeared for more than three years. She has appeared as a regular on such television shows as *Dinah, NBC Bandstand, Girl Talk, The Merv Griffin Show, Liar's Club*, and *The Stan Kahn Show*. Recent television appearances include recurring roles on *Diff'rent Strokes* and *Punky Brewster*, and she has been seen on *Murder She Wrote* and *Crazy Like A Fox*, among others.

Film credits include *Max Dugan Returns, Grease, Grease II, Splash,* and *Splash II.* Dody is also the author of *Mourning In A Funny Hat*, the story of a widow's struggle to develop independence following the death of her husband, which starred Shirley Booth in a stock company tour. She penned, produced, and starred in a one-hour documentary film entitled *Women, Women, Women*, which takes a comedic look at women's struggle for emancipation.

ROBERT GOULET

"It takes training, like anything else in this world."

Robert Goulet

I don't know who Robert Goulet really is, but he's progressing continually. The voice itself is basically there, to a certain extent. But if I had not taken serious training, I could be part of a Glee Club today, with possibly my own plumbing shop somewhere. I might even be Vice President, but I wouldn't be able to sing with the controlled sound I now have. I'd be singing in my throat, squeezing away. I had a scholarship to the Conservatory of Music in Toronto when I lived in Canada. The last teacher I had taught me how to produce the sound which is necessary to create some of those notes. Yes, it takes training, like anything else in this world.

I had done a lot of work in Canada. I did theatre and television, and for three years, I was the host of a national network TV show which aired 7:30 P.M., Sunday nights, just before Ed Sullivan. During that time, they were looking for a Lancelot for the new musical *Camelot*. They checked everywhere. You know the routine, when they can't find exactly what they want.

Well, I was on a holiday in Bermuda, playing golf with a few friends. As a joke, I left word on my answering machine where I was staying in Bermuda. After golf one day, there was a message from this Mr. Newborn, in New York. I called him back and he said, "Can you come to New York and audition for Lerner and Loewe?" I said, "No, 'cause I'm working. I'm going back to Toronto in two days to do my TV show, and there's no time to get to New York."

So I went back to Toronto and told the stage director about it. I expected him to say, 'Are you kidding? We only have one day to rehearse. You're not going anywhere." But he shocked me and said, "Go, you deserve the chance." I went and lost my luggage at the airport. I auditioned in jeans and a tee-shirt. Moss Hart said, "I see you've come prepared for action." I sang and they gave me the job, that minute.

That was the beginning for me in the States.

I just toured with *South Pacific* for two years. I never saw it done on the stage before I did it. The role itself has no humor, but in a couple of spots, I bring a little bit of humor to it. I like getting laughs. Actually, whatever you play, if you do it honestly, the audience will accept it as it is.

ROBERT GOULET

On December 3rd, 1960, Robert Goulet burst upon the Broadway stage in Lerner and Loewe's immortal classic *Camelot*. As Lancelot, he became the most romantic hero on the Broadway stage. Many appearances on the *Ed Sullivan Show* garnered him other television offers, plus recording and film contracts.

Born in Lawrence, Massachusetts, he moved to Edmonton, Alberta, Canada, after his father's death. Following high school, he soloed with The Edmonton, Alberta Symphony Orchestra, did a two-year stint as a radio announcer, and was awarded a singing scholarship to the Royal Conservatory of Music, University of Toronto, Ontario.

The Grammy for Best New Artist was awarded him in 1962. Of the more than forty albums he recorded, mostly for the Columbia label, *My Love, Forgive Me,* in 1966, earned him the distinction of a gold album. Twenty years later, he and his.wife Vera formed their own recording company, ROVE, and he recorded his latest album *Won't You Dance With This Man*.

Robert has displayed versatile talents, dividing his time between night clubs, television and films, but always returning to his first love, the theatre. Besides *Camelot* in 1960, his other stage roles include *I Do, I Do* (1970); *Camelot* (in 1975 as King Arthur); *Carousel* (1979); *On A Clear Day* (1980); *Kiss Me Kate* (1981); and *South Pacific* (1986). In 1968 he earned the most precious and coveted theatre award, the Tony, for Best Actor in *The Happy Time*.

He has performed at the White House for three Presidents: Lyndon B. Johnson, Richard Nixon, and Ronald Reagan. He has also performed for Queen Elizabeth at several Royal Command Performances.

RONNY GRAHAM

"When I was a kid, I stuttered like mad, but I was determined to be a comic."

Ronny Graham

I started as a writer when I was eight years old, way back in the third grade. There was a Triple A safety magazine, and I wrote a poem for it that they published. My poem:

"Little Johnny Carelessness was walking
'cross the street
He didn't look to left or right, where he put
his feet
An auto fast came running by and hit
poor Johnny's leg
And now poor Johnny, to this day is walk-
ing on a peg."

I've always felt tugs and pulls to go into different directions. That's how I found out I'm multi-talented. I'd write for a while, then I'd think, I want to act.

My association with Mel Brooks has always been important to me. I knew him thirty-six years ago when we both were starting out. He was low man on the totem pole, then writing for *Your Show Of Shows*. I've written with him and worked with him many times.

When I was a kid, I stuttered like mad, but I was determined to be a comic. I started by making fun of myself. When I got out of the army, in 1946, I joined a Jazz Band. People started to ask more for me and my comedy songs than the jazz, so I left and did a comedy solo act.

I was working in a night club in New York when Imogene Coca brought this Broadway producer, Leonard Sillman, to see me perform. She's been sort of my good luck charm all my life. That's how I got my first big break — in Leonard Sillman's *New Faces of 1952*, as did Eartha Kitt, Paul Lynde, and Alice Ghostley.

My first straight play was *The Tender Trap* with Robert Preston and Kim Hunter. The first day of rehearsal, I was scared out of my wits. Robert Preston started giving me acting lessons, but I was nearly fired, 'till I lost my fright and settled in.

The most rewarding day of my life was when my grammar school had a Ronny Graham Day. All my old teachers were there, and having them honor me was as good as my Tony Award. I did get a Tony for *New Faces* and a Tony nomination as a writer for *Bravo, Giovanni.*

On TV, I've been on Johnny Carson's show over fifty times, and I've done commercials as "Mr. Dirt," which got me tremendous recognition. They even had a "Mr. Dirt Day" for me at Notre Dame. I've written for and performed in films and in clubs, but nothing thrills me more than working in theatre with a live audience laughing.

I always have a new project. Currently, I'm writing a musical based on the life of Jennie Grossinger, who founded Grossinger's Hotel, in the Catskill Mountains. Not bad for an "alter cocker!"

RONNY GRAHAM

Ronny Graham is a veteran of the stage and screen, having starred, written, and directed in virtually all varieties of comedy and drama. His more recent stage credits are *The Value Of Names,* a new play directed by Gordon Hunt, and *Jokers,* a new musical. In past years, he appeared on Broadway in *The Tender Trap,* co-starred in *The Recruiting Officer,* and wrote songs and skits for *The Shoestring Revue* Off-Broadway. In 1962, he was nominated for a Tony Award for his lyrics for *Bravo, Giovanni.* He replaced Julius Monk as the Impresario of the Upstairs of the Downstairs where he produced, directed, co-wrote, and starred in two reviews and directed the musical *Money.*

He has teamed up with Mel Brooks on many of Brooks' films, including *Spaceballs,* in which he starred and co-wrote; *To Be Or Not To Be* (which he co-authored), and *History Of The World, Part I,* for which he composed the Inquisition Song. Ronny made his theatrical debut on Broadway in *New*

Faces Of 1952, in which he co-starred with Alice Ghostley, Robert Clary, Eartha Kitt, Paul Lynde, and Carol Lawrence and also composed most of the songs and sketches. On television, Graham received a coveted Emmy Award for his TV role in *Mike Royko At Best*. He has made more than 50 appearances on *The Tonight Show* with Johnny Carson, for which he wrote original music and lyrics for each show.

SCOTT HAMILTON

"Sports really isn't about money or commercial endorsements. It's about pure loving what you can be."

Scott Hamilton

I started skating, just to skate, to give me something to do, and it was something I could do well. I had an intestinal paralyzation problem when I was young; I couldn't absorb my food, so I didn't grow for several years. I picked up skating very quickly, and it was something that allowed me to compete with kids that were larger and stronger than I was. I enjoyed it and I just kept at it. It's like you get to the first little plateau and then the next one, and the next one, and the next one, and pretty soon I was in the senior level, trying to make the Olympic team; and it's been great.

I'm not really sure, 'cause it sounds kind of dramatic, but it definitely gave me a direction; it gave me something that really made me feel good. The better you feel about yourself, the better you feel physically. So it's a tribute to ice skating, for improving my health.

Unlike some other ice skaters, I never took dance class. I come from a small town in Ohio, and people there don't always understand the need for ballet classes to become an ice skater. I played hockey for three years, because of the peer pressure involved in figure skating.

Actually, dance didn't interest me as much. I wanted to be an athlete. I wanted to be more gymnastic on the ice. Skating is a show-off sport. The entire thing is how well you can show-off to get the points or the applause. If you stick with your personality, that's where your better skaters excel, because it's genuine when you see someone basically bare their soul.

The plane crash in the early 1960's took the entire United States figure skating team and decimated our entire international involvement. It really hurt the whole Olympic skating program. It was a tragic thing to happen, and it brought things into redevelopment. "Out of the ashes comes the phoenix." We had a lot of success in the ladies' competition; but in the men's, although we'd always win the world championship, we just couldn't win the gold medal in the Olympics until I was fortunate enough to win in 1984 (and again in 1988).

Then it came down to: I'd been world champion in 1981, '82, '83, and '84, and then I won the Olympic gold medal. There really wasn't anything left for me to do in the amateur ranks, and I was broke. I decided it was time to turn "pro" and see if I could create a career and develop as a performer and entertainer.

I got involved in many kinds of productions, traditional ice shows in arenas, as well as new shows like *Broadway On Ice*.

So, I've had the opportunity to learn many different styles of skating and choreography, and different ways of presenting it — not just as athletics, but as art entertainment as well. In a theatre, everything is quicker, tighter, more danceable and more concentrated. You need more than just athletic ability to pull it off. You need the emotion.

As a young person (I didn't want to say small person), I tend to get into trouble every now and then. I don't enjoy being in a show unless occasionally I can pull some mischief.

I'm not sure what I'll do when I can't skate anymore. I'm kind of looking around . . . But, I love to perform. You know, every athlete wants to be an actor.

One thing I really care about is "The Special Olympics." It's a terrific program. It's sports as it is meant to be; personal excellence. Sports really isn't about money or commercial endorsements. It's about pure loving what you can be, and to be the best you can be, regardless of what anyone else does.

I guess that's my credo, too: The love you put into the sport.

SCOTT HAMILTON

Scott Hamilton has been the world's most celebrated male figure skater since 1981, when he won the first of eight consecutive National and World titles. The Olympic Gold Medal he won in Sarajevo, Yugoslavia, in 1984, was the first won by an American since 1960. By 1980, he was good enough to capture third place in the National competition and win a berth on the U.S. Olympic squad. In addition, he earned a solid fifth-place finish at the 1980 Olympics at Lake

Placid. Then, in March, 1981, Scott's dazzling free-skating program at the World Championships enabled him to win the title.

Later the same year, he took an individual Gold Medal at the first Skate America tournament and was voted Male Athlete of the Year by the United States Olympic Committee. Scott held on to his national and world titles in '82 and '83. He won fifteen straight championships and then the Gold Medal in men's figure skating at the 1984 Winter Olympics in Sarajevo. He went on to score a stunning victory at the World Championships in Ottawa, Canada.

In April, 1984, Scott turned professional; the Ice Capades secured his superstar talents for two years. In September, 1987, he was nominated for the first "Olympic Spirit Award," given for the 1984 Winter Games. During 1986 and 1987, audiences saw Scott perform in his own *Scott Hamilton's America Tour, Stars On Ice*, co-headlining with Dorothy Hamill, and the national touring proscenium stage production of *Festival On Ice*. Additionally, he is a frequent celebrity guest player on television game shows, has guest-starred with Emma Samms on the ABC Television special *An Olympic, Calgary Christmas* and hosted the Home Box Office *Salute To Dorothy Hamill*.

In March, 1988, Scott Hamilton received perhaps the second most important award in his career, the Jacques Favart Award. A most prestigious honor, it has been bestowed upon only four other Olympic athletes in history. He not only starred in, but produced his first theatrical production for the world famous marine life park of Sea World in San Diego, California. Mr. Hamilton also enters his fifth year of service as one of the most colorful and articulate sports commentators on the CBS Television Network.

JULIE HARRIS

"If I could go back and do it again, I might have gone to England to study, where I would have gotten classical training.

Julie Harris

In my teens I learned by osmosis, watching the theatre companies that came through Detroit. Then, I did go to school for three summers at The Perry Mansfeld Theatre Workshop in Steamboat Springs, Colorado. Many great dancers, actors, musicians and composers started in this workshop. The theatre they built was named for me, "The Julie

Harris Theatre."

My first professional job was in 1945, in a play called *It's A Gift*. On the fifth day of rehearsal, when an actor can be let go, I was fired, but rehired two days later. The playwright liked me and had confidence in me, although the producers thought I was too inexperienced. And I was. But what a catastrophic experience for a beginner. The envelope came on the fifth day and it said, "Your services are terminated." Fortunately, I was rehired and did open with the play.

I've never stopped doing theatre. Even the seven years I was on *Knot's Landing* I did theatre. I did an original play during that time called *Under The Ilex*, which Charles Nelson Reilly directed, at The Long Wharf Theatre. I did *Bronte*, which I still travel with. All the one-woman plays I've done, I've selected myself. Charles Nelson Reilly said I was obsessed with Emily Dickinson. Perhaps. My obsession led to *The Belle of Amherst*, which Charles also directed.

What established me on Broadway was playing twelve-year-old "Frankie Adams" in *Member Of The Wedding*. Sally Bowles in *I Am A Camera* got me my first Tony Award. I'm most proud of my honorary Masters of Arts degree bestowed by Smith College, which was prompted by Joan of Arc in *The Lark*.

I got to duplicate my roles in *Member Of The Wedding* and *I Am A Camera* for the motion pictures and *The Lark* for television.

My resume shows a succession of colorful roles; each different and I hope, memorable.

As for the perfect play, that would have to be *Driving Miss Daisy*. It won the Pulitzer Prize. It's a poem, a cantanta with a great part, that of author Alfred Uhry's grandmother. Here I had a real story, and was able to research it. That's what I advise, for any real play. To help me in the role, I was given a little black felt hat, which his grandmother wore. I, too, wore it for the duration of the play.

In the spring of 1990, I'll be doing a new play by Donald Freed called *Is He Still Dead?* It's the story of James Joyce and his wife. Charles Nelson Reilly will direct.

I keep going on, but if I could go back and do it again, I might have gone to England to study, where I would have gotten classical training. This is a time of a little more freedom. How lucky, for those starting out.

JULIE HARRIS

Julie Harris made her Broadway debut in *It's A Gift* on Monday, March 12, 1945. She then appeared with Britain's Old Vic Company during its fabled 1946 visit, appearing in *Henry IV, Part II* and *Oedipus*. Next came a revival of Synge's *The Playboy Of The Western World* with Burgess Meredith, a chance to understudy Bambi Linn in *Alice In Wonderland*, then an appearance with Michael Redgrave, playing one of the witches in *Macbeth*. By the time the young native of Grosse Pointe, Michigan, appeared in *Sundown Beach* and *The Young And Fair*, she was widely recognized as a promising newcomer. But it was not until 1950 and Harold Clurman's production of Carson McCullers' *Member Of The Wedding* that the actress, playing an isolated twelve-year-old, Frankie Adams, gained genuine prominence.

The first of Ms. Harris' five Tony Awards — the highest number ever accumulated by a performer — came as a result of her next Broadway role, the free-spirited Sally Bowles in John Van Druten's *I Am A Camera* in 1952. The second Tony arrived as a result of the actress' work as St. Joan in Lillian Hellman's adaptation of Jean Anouilh's *The Lark* in 1956. The plays which followed — *The Country Wife, The Warm Peninsula, A Shot In The Dark, Little Moon Of Alban, Marathon 33, And Miss Reardon Drinks A Little, The*

Au Pair Man, and the musical *Skyscraper*, based on Elmer Rice's *Dream Girl* — served to indicate her incredible range. She played Juliet for the Stratford Ontario Shakespeare Festival and Ophelia in a New York Shakespeare Festival production of *Hamlet*

Ms. Harris' third Tony came with *Forty Carats* in 1969, followed four years later in 1973 by another in recognition of her work as Mary Todd Lincoln in *The Last Of Mrs. Lincoln* by James Prideaux. She appeared in a new Prideaux play, *Tusitala*, as Fannie Osbourne Stevenson, the wife of author Robert Louis Stevenson. Ms. Harris' fifth and most recent Tony was awarded in 1977 for the performance as the poet Emily Dickinson in William Luce's one-character play, *The Belle Of Amherst*. The play, directed by Charles Nelson Reilly, was a triumph both nationwide and on Broadway. Her recording of it won a 1977 Grammy Award.

The actress recreated two of her most outstanding stage roles for the movies: Frankie in *Member Of The Wedding*, for which she was nominated for an Academy Award, and Sally in *I Am A Camera*. The film role for which she is best known, however, is Abra, opposite James Dean in Elia Kazan's screen version of the John Steinbeck novel, *East Of Eden*. Her other films include *The Truth About Women, Requiem For A Heavyweight, Harper, The People Next Door, Reflections In A Golden Eye*, and, a favorite of the actress, *The Hiding Place*.

She has been nominated nine times for television's Emmy Awards, winning for *Little Moon Of Alban* (1958-59 season) and *Victoria Regina* (1961-62 season). Other outstanding television appearances were in *Ethan Frome, The Lark, Pygmalion, A Doll's House, The Power And The Glory*, and *Johnny Belinda*. She recently completed seven years as Lilimae Clements on *Knot's Landing* on CBS' prime time schedule. When the series was in hiatus, Ms. Harris found time to play Dora Carrington in Clyde Talmage's *Under*

The Ilex and for a second one-woman work by playwright Luce, *Bronte*, subtitled *A Solo Portrait Of Charlotte Bronte*. Ms. Harris appeared opposite Jason Robards in the HBO-TV special, *The Christmas Wife*.

KIM HUNTER

"To follow any method absolutely blindly and rigidly makes no sense at all."

Kim Hunter

I grew up in Miami Beach and graduated from Miami Beach High School. Somewhere around the tenth grade, one of my chums in school said, "My mother and father are moving in with this older couple. We're sharing a house, and she's a drama coach." My ears pricked up because I was an avid movie fan at that time. I was beginning to think this was something I wanted to do, and so I started studying with

Charmine Lantoff. We got highly individual attention, with only three or four in the class. We also studied fencing, voice and eurythmics. Charmine was responsible for my first jobs, starting with "little theatre" work. Then she started "The Old Mill Playhouse" in Flat Rock, North Carolina, which today is North Carolina's State Theatre. I was up there for a couple of summers as the resident ingenue.

I met "the method" when I got to New York City, which is, I think, a way of working when your instinct isn't serving you. To follow any method absolutely blindly and rigidly makes no sense to me at all. Every actor is different and responds to different things in different ways. My method is to make it as true and as honest as I can. I try to find the character through myself as much as I can. Although there are all kinds of exercises to stimulate the imagination, to stimulate the senses, I think actually doing it on the job is the best training.

I was "under contract" to David O. Selznick when he and Irene were still married. When Irene, Tennessee Williams, and Elia Kazan started to cast *A Streetcar Named Desire*, she noticed in the *New York Times* that I was playing *Claudia* on the summer stock circuit and said to herself (so she told me later), "If the girl is now acting on stage, maybe she's pretty good. Let's get her to read for the role of Stella." That's how I got to make my Broadway debut and to eventually do the film, for which I was awarded the Academy Award.

I had a lot of trouble making the transition to film. They told me when I went into my first film that the camera exaggerates everything, so if you don't do anything, you're going to be fine. My first film was also Mark Robson's first as a director. The both of us were very nervous. But he was an absolute darling and he'd say, "We better do it over again," and I'd think, "Oh, I'm twitching or something." He said, "No, you look as if you're embalmed." That's how it came out in my effort to do nothing.

Well, I gradually understood you can do what comes naturally in film, too. It just doesn't have to project to the last row in the balcony. One of the interesting things about film is the concentration it requires. You cannot be not alive for a second. Whereas film is a realistic medium, theatre is unrealistic. There's no way you can get on a stage and say this is actually happening. The audience is absolutely aware of it.

I'm a firm believer in training. That's how I started. One must develop the voice and the body to make it all do what you want it to do and what the role requires you to do. Still, it's not until you finally get on the stage do you really learn.

KIM HUNTER

Kim Hunter made her Broadway debut as Stella Kowalski in *A Streetcar Named Desire* in December, 1947, for which she won both the Donaldson and Critics' Awards. She later won an Academy Award, *Look* Magazine Award, and Hollywood Foreign Correspondents' Golden Globe for her performance in the film version of the play.

In addition to *Streetcar*, some of her films include *Stairway To Heaven, Deadline: USA, Lilith, The Swimmer, The Kindred,* and the first three of the highly successful *Planet Of The Apes* quintet, in which she played the chimpanzee psychiatrist, Dr. Zira.

Ms. Hunter has appeared on hundreds of television programs — from the early days of "live TV to the present — and was nominated for an Emmy Award for her performance as "Crazy Annie" on *Baretta* as well as for her role of Nola Madison on *Edge Of Night.*

Her numerous stage appearances include starring roles in *Darkness At Noon, The Children's Hour, The Tender Trap, Write Me A Murder, Weekend*, the revival of *The Women, To*

Grandmother's House We Go — all on Broadway. Her favorite roles in regional theatre productions include Emily Dickinson in *The Belle Of Amherst*, Eleanor of Aquitaine in *The Lion In Winter*, Madame Ranevskaya in *The Cherry Orchard*, and Mrs. Alving in *Ghosts*. In the past few years, she has played Linda Loman in *Death Of A Salesman* at the Stratford Shakespeare Festival in Ontario and at the Coconut Grove Playhouse, for which she won Florida's Carbonnell Award, Vinnie in *Life With Father* with Jose Ferrer, also at the Coconut Grove, Mama in *Faulkner's Bicycle* at the Yale Repertory Theatre in New Haven and at the Joyce Theatre's American Theatre Exchange in New York City, and Fanny in *Painting Churches* at the Hartman Theatre in Stanford, Connecticut.

In the fall of 1987, she played Theresa in Graham Reid's *Remembrance* at the Huntington Theatre in Boston. Since then, she has played Mrs. Whitefield in the Roundabout Theatre's production of *Man And Superman*, New York City; Fonsia in *The Gin Game* at the Fulton Opera House in Lancaster, Pennsylvania; and Jennie Woodson in *A Murder Of Crows* at the South Street Theatre on Theatre Row, New York City, Fall, 1988. In 1989, she appeared in *Cross Of Fire* — a four-hour/two-part miniseries for NBC and also a theatrical film, *Two Evil Eyes* —release date in 1990.

As a side note, Ms. Hunter made her musical debut in October, 1986, as Fonsia in *Jokers*, a musical version of *The Gin Game*, at the Goodspeed Theatre in Chester, Connecticut. She is also the author of an autobiograhical cookbook entitled *Loose In The Kitchen*.

JUDY KAYE

"I didn't want to be anyone's understudy. It's such a heartbreaking job."

Judy Kaye

My story is a fairy tale which is as wonderful and magical as it sounds, like it should be.

Once upon a time, I had the small but semi-rewarding part as Agnes the maid in *On The Twentieth Century*, and I was Madeline Kahn's understudy. I had turned down the job several times, 'cause I didn't want to be anyone's understudy. It's such a heartbreaking job. But somebody's got to do it . . . so I did.

We were out of town in Boston for about four or five weeks, and I was learning the show; but we didn't have any understudy rehearsals. You don't have them until you open on Broadway and the show is secure, so I was on my own. Luckily, I wasn't banned from any of the rehearsals, which can happen with some stars. The main thing is I listened to what director Hal Prince was saying, and I took notes. We came back to New York in a snowstorm and opened.

On March 6, 1978, I went to the gym to work out and got to the theatre five minutes late. Everyone knew I was going on but me. I wasn't anywhere near a phone all day. Who needed me? They said, "You're going on." Clothes were thrown on me. Wigs were thrown on me. All the stuff I had been doing in my little room, like if I ever get a chance to do it, I think I'll do this, or that. When I went on, all that went away. I just went out with enthusiasm and shock and adrenalin and instinct.

I went on nine times for Madeline in a five-week period, and then she decided to leave. Instead of going to a "name," they asked me if I wanted to do it and to go through the publicity that goes with it. It was just great.

Prior to this, I had been working for a long time . . . I won't tell you how many years. After this amazing experience, many new doors opened for me. It put me on another plateau, where not only does the price go up, but the quality of the offers and the quality of the material, as well as the opportunity to work all over the country.

This was the one time where fantasy actually was not as good as reality.

JUDY KAYE

Judy Kaye received the Theatre World Award, the Los Angles Drama Critic's Circle Award, and the Drama Desk Nomination for her work as the platinum blonde Lily Garland in *On The Twentieth Century*, both on Broadway and on tour with Rock Hudson and Imogene Coca. Ms. Kaye starred on Broadway in *The Moony Shapiro Songbook, Oh, Brother,* and as Rizzo in the long-running *Grease*. She played Hodel in four companies of *Fiddler On The Roof*, sang the role of Mary Magdalene in five companies of *Jesus Christ, Superstar* and Agnes in *I Do, I Do* opposite John Davidson for the Dallas Summer Musicals.

Ms. Kaye has starred as Lilli Vanessi in *Kiss Me, Kate*, Pistache in *Can-Can* for the Saint Louis Muny Opera, and as LaLume in the Canadian Opera's production of *Kismet*. She has played Julie Jordan in *Carousel*, Maria in *The Sound Of Music* opposite both Noel Harrison and George Peppard, Nellie in *South Pacific*, Annie in *Annie, Get Your Gun*, Aldonza in *Man Of La Mancha*, and Mrs. Lovett in *Sweeney Todd*. She performed in the production of *Side By Side By Sondheim* opposite Larry Kert, Helen Gallagher, and George Rose, and created the role of Molly Molloy in *Windy City*, and *Berlinto Broadway*. Her off-Broadway credits include Ellen in *It's Love, Four To Make Two*, and appearing in Victor Herbert's *Eileen* and *Sweethearts*, and both Jerome Kern's *Leave It To Jane* and *Sweet Adeline*.

Judy was featured as Alan King's daughter in the film *Just Tell Me What You Want*. Her TV credits include guest starring roles on *Kojak*, a regular role on *Mr. Deeds Goes To Town* and on *The Doctors*. Ms. Kaye's critically acclaimed night club act has played both New York and Los Angeles.

Judy was born in Phoenix, Arizona, before attending UCLA where she was the recipient of several acting and musical honors including winning the Frank Sinatra Music Award.

She received a Tony Award as Best Featured Actress in a Musical and a Drama Desk Nomination for her work in *Phantom Of The Opera*. Recent credits include the world premiere of *Desire Under The Elms*, an opera based on the Eugene O'Neill drama, and Babe in *The Pajama Game*. She recently recorded two albums, *Kismet* and *What About Love* for That's Entertainment Records.

LAINIE KAZAN

"We all learn as actors that the least is better, that less is more."

Lainie Kazan

I studied speech therapy at Hofstra University, Long Island, New York, and became a speech therapist, all the while studying singing; and I credit Joseph K. Scott, my voice teacher, for my success as a singer. He was my "Guru." I was only nineteen when I met him, and he was a very young man then, too. I was like a guinea pig since I was so accessible and so ready to learn. Everything he taught me was physiologically correct for me — not something a lot of other voice teachers had told me to do, whether it be squeeze this, or push up that. His was a method of great relaxation, of learning to sing by doing as little as possible. That's what we all learn as actors, that the least is better, that less is more.

He was amazing for me. I studied with him exclusively, and he'd always come to my performances and travel with me. Mine was a classical approach to vocal training. That's what got me through two shows a night in clubs, where I'd sing for two to three hours.

I studied drama with Sanford Meisner and then with Lee Strasberg for five years. I'm a life member of The Actors Studio.

My theatre career got started by understudying Barbra Streisand in the musical *Funny Girl* and getting to go on for her, twice in one day.

My film career began through an old college friend, Francis Ford Coppola. He came in to hear me sing in my night club in Los Angeles and offered me a role in a film called *One From The Heart*. He put the "Midas Touch" on me, 'cause that was the start of my acting career in films.

Mel Brooks wanted me for the journalist in *My Favorite Year*, but I wanted the Jewish mama. He thought I was crazy. But, I said, "Let me read for this." I mean, I knew that lady so well. I grew up on Ocean Parkway in Brooklyn, sitting on the benches, with these women.

So, I had a friend do my make-up and my hair, and I came in dressed for the role and got the part. Unfortunately, what happens when you do a memorable role like that is people believe you really look like that, and those are the only roles you get offered. I didn't mind doing it again, but I finally said, enough is enough.

If I were starting all over again, I would take a business course. I only understood the show part of show business, when I was growing up in the sixties and seventies. It was a pretty vulnerable time for me, and I had a lot to learn. I became a pawn in a lot of very manipulative men's hands.

Recently, my daughter, who sings like a gospel singer, asked me if I'd mind if she made a career of singing. Of course, I said I'd be delighted. Singing has given me the joy and the pleasure and the fulfillment for my life. A lot of people who come to see me, and know I work sixteen, eighteen hours a day, say I'm crazy. But when you're creating art, there is no limit; there are no boundaries. It's not work, it's sheer and absolute joy. The labor is a labor of love, as long as you can be relaxed. When you do it for yourself, it's so much more appealing to everybody else. If you're trying so hard to entertain, somehow it comes off as not interesting. The most interesting thing about you is you; and isn't it fun to love your work?

LAINIE KAZAN

In 1981, Lainie rekindled an earlier friendship with Francis Ford Coppola, and he offered her the role of Teri Garr's roommate in *One From The Heart*, thus launching her film career. In 1983, she received a Golden Globe Award for her portrayal of the Jewish mother in *My Favorite Year* with Peter O'Toole. She has starred in numerous other feature films such as *Delta Force* with Shelly Winters, Disney's *Natty Gann*, Steven Spielberg's *Harry And The Hendersons*, and the cult classic *Lust In The Dust* with Tab Hunter and Divine.

For her 1986 performance in Showtimes's acclaimed *Paper Chase* series with John Houseman (Lainie's entrance into serious television), she received an ACE nomination. Lainie co-starred with Patty Duke in the new Fox-TV series *Karen's Song* and played Howie Mandel's mother in the successful television series *St. Elsewhere*. She has also guest-starred on *Hotel, Columbo*, and *Too Close For Comfort*, as well as almost every variety and talk show, including Johnny Carson's *Tonight Show*.

Lainie was first catapulted to fame when, as understudy to Barbra Streisand in the Broadway musical production of *Funny Girl*, she went on for the indisposed star. Lainie has since originated the role of Gittel Mosca in the musical *Seesaw* and the role of Crystal in Clare Booth Luce's *The Women*. She has also performed in New York in *Jacques Brel Is Alive And Well And Living In Paris* and *Man Of La Mancha*. Her regional credits include *On A Clear Day You Can See Forever, Who's Afraid Of Virginia Woolf?, The House Of Blue Leaves, Orpheus Descending*, and *The Rose Tattoo*. Lainie has recorded five albums, including *The Chanteuse Is Loose*, which she produced on her own label, and was the recipient of the Best New Singer of the Year Award of 1970. She has acted as proprietor of her own nightclubs, Lainie's Room in Los Angeles and Lainie's Room East in New York City. She is a Life Member of the Actor's Studio. She currently resides in Los Angeles with her daughter Jennifer.

RICHARD KLINE

"The reality of acting is bringing your own personality to it."

Richard Kline

If I were starting again, I guess I'd still do it the same way. I studied not just drama in school, but the history of drama; and I studied directing and scenic design. I went to Northwestern and to Queens College and got my degree. I think if a young person starting out wanted to be in the theatre, they should try everything as I did. They might take a directing class and say, "Hey, I like directing better than acting."

I like to direct, too, and every now and then, to teach, as I have at "The Burt Reynolds Institute." I taught the interns there the techniques of auditioning for theatre and for television and the fundamentals of acting.

A particularly tremendous experience for me was playing Henry V at the Folger Shakespeare Theatre in Washington, D.C. We were reviewed by a visiting English travel critic. He said, "Should you be in the Washington, D.C. area, do go and see *Henry V* starring Richard Kline I can report the role is in very capable hands." Now, an English critic, to say that!

I had never done any television, but a lot of my friends were. At that time, Peter Strauss was doing the mini-series *Rich Man, Poor Man*, and my friend Henry Winkler was starring on *Happy Days*. "Wow," I said, "there's success, riches and fame to be made out there." Henry, who had done theatre in Yale and off-Broadway in New York, said, "Come out here. There's a lot more volume of work to be had."

The first show I got was *The Mary Tyler Moore Show*. The word got out that I did comedy. So much for all the drama I did in New York. Then I did three *Maude's* with Bea Arthur, which was an incredible experience for me, being around that lady. I owe a lot of my comedic timing to her. Then, I got lucky and got on *Three's Company*. I realized you can earn a very nice living doing episodic TV, but it doesn't mean you'll instantly become a star.

You asked if I play myself in theatre and television. Well, the reality of acting is bringing your own personality to it. You have to find the life of the character and say, "Would the character do this?" I might, but he may not. So you have to find where to draw the line. But to succeed in this business, the bottom line is . . . determination!

RICHARD KLINE

Richard Kline received rave reviews in Los Angeles at the Coronet Theatre where he co-starred with David Morse in the play *How I Got That Story*, playing 20 different roles in a chameleon-like performance. *Variety* stated, "It's a tour-de-force." He also received critical acclaim for these roles at the prestigious Kennedy Center in Washington, D.C.

With a Master's Degree in Theatre from Northwestern, his other stage credits include the National Tour of *The Rothschilds, Troilius and Cressida* for Joseph Papp, *Child's Play, Chemin De Fer*, the title role in *Henry V, Death Of A Salesman, Come Blow Your Horn* and *The Sunshine Boys.* His talent as a singer was showcased early in his career in such productions as *Do I Hear A Waltz, The Fantasticks*, and, of course, *The Rothschilds.*

Richard played eight seasons on the highly successful ABC sitcom *Three's Company* as Larry Dallas, the upstairs neighbor and perpetual bachelor. Mr. Kline appeared on *Hill Street Blues* and his other guest starring roles for television include *The Mary Tyler Moore Show, Eight Is Enough, Maude* and *Fernwood Tonight.* He currently appears in a recurring role on *It's A Living* and recently completed a Group W Productions pilot entitled *Together Again.*

BERNIE KOPELL

"The actor's tools are adaptability, because you're not going to be cast all the time as you would like to be."

Bernie Kopell

I had very formal training at New York University. So formal that I got hung up for five years with a very "speechified" approach and nothing happened. People on the West Coast had no idea what to do with me. Finally, I sort of relaxed in "arena" theatre with "The Players Ring," which was tremendously valuable in my developing a sort of intimate style.

I think what happens when you start out with a very strong Brooklyn accent, which I had, you try to compensate, and you sound like a machine. You have to strike a happy medium.

Learning accents was a necessity for me. Casting directors would say, "What are we going to do with you? You're not ugly enough to be a 'heavy' and you're not handsome enough to be a leading man." So, I sat there with a lot of time on my hands, not being cast, thinking, what can I do. For want of something to do, I found myself playing with accents. There was an audition that was a turning point for me. I read for "Pablo," a Latin "heavy" on the soap *Brighter Day* and ended up playing him for three months.

Now, I was on a very strange departure. I was acting, but I was playing very far away from myself, and that set the pattern for me. I did nothing but Latinos for five years. I was typecast and played *The Danny Kaye Show, The Jack Benny Show, My Favorite Martian* and *The Flying Nun*, always as a Latin.

The actor's tools are adaptability, because you're not going to be cast all the time as you would like to be. It's your obligation to yourself, and to your profession, to extend every possible tangent of yourself. Can you sing, dance or direct? Ask yourself, "What have I got that I can maximize, that I can have fun with?" What you enjoy is what you're going to do the best.

So, always be prepared and try to maintain your best standard of excellence.

BERNIE KOPELL

On the stage, his credits include A. R. Gurney's *The Dining Room* on the 1983 Westport Circuit and playing Jason in

Bernard Slade's *Romantic Comedy*. In Los Angeles, he performed at the Players Ring Theatre productions of *Dark At The Top Of The Stairs, Majority Of One* and *Wedding Breakfast*. He also portrayed the role of Artie Strauss in *Compulsion*. At 24 years old, he appeared as the 80-year-old Rabbi in *The Lonely Ship*, with the great Yiddish actor Maurice Schwartz.

A turning point in Bernie's career occurred when Leonard Stern saw him as the shy Russian peddler in the title role of the hit comedy *The 49th Cousin*, which was held over for a nine-month run. That visit resulted in Bernie's being cast in the hit TV series *Get Smart* in the role of the villainous Siegfried, the head of KAOS. His television career culminated in the role of Dr. Adam Bricker, which he played for nine years on the ABC-TV hit series *Love Boat*.

Having gained his wide audience as a romantic leading man — The Doctor on *Love Boat* — was quite a remarkable feat considering that most of his roles were character roles for much of the first 20 years of his career. He predominantly played Latins in the first four years, evolving to German, Russian, Japanese and Chinese. Early on, he developed a mastery for accents, which he utilized on *The Danny Kaye Show, The Jack Benny Show, The Steve Allen Show, The Flying Nun* and *My Favorite Martian*.

From 1966-77 he was a regular on two series simultaneously: *Get Smart* and *The Marlo Thomas Show*. Occasionally during that time, he appeared in yet a third series, as Louie Palucci on *The Doris Day Show*. In 1966, he played Howard Wagner, the boss' son who fires Willie Loman, in the acclaimed CBS Special *Death Of A Salesman*, starring Lee J. Cobb. On *Bewitched*, Bernie was "resident stock company," appearing on demand in seemingly countless roles including the 100-year-old Apothecary, the Viennese Psychiatrist, the Hippie and —himself! He also has starred in the major motion pictures *The Oregon Trail* with Fred MacMurray, *The Thrill Of It All* with Doris Day and Jim Garner, Arthur Hiller's *Wheeler Dealers* and Bill Naud's *God Bless You, Uncle Sam!*

CLEO LAINE

"Don't imitate. Don't sing like anybody else. Be yourself."

Cleo Laine

A lot of people ask how I can do all I do, and tour as well. The answer is you have to love it. If you don't love it, don't do it. I'm a "gypsy." I always have been and always will be. I don't like to know what I'm going to be doing in four years time — like opera singers, for instance They know what they're going to sing, what productions they're going to be in. That would disturb me intensely.

It all started for me in Britain. I never had any other

thought in my head than that I would be on the stage. My father was a singer, but not a professional singer. He sang on the streets during the depression years. He had to earn money some way. I came from this musical Victorian family. We entertained each other. And although I had lots and lots of jobs before I became professional, I knew in my heart the stage was going to be it.

I auditioned. It became my hobby. Nobody ever wanted me, but I kept on. I entered talent competitions. I never ever won, but I still went into them. One day I auditioned for the man I eventually married. He heard something all the others never did. What it was, I don't know. This was still in Britain where he had a jazz group. I had been auditioning for commercial groups, who really wanted the current singer of the day, who sang like Doris Day. According to my husband, I didn't sound like anybody else, and he gave me the job.

Now, I realize, that's the answer. Don't imitate. Don't sing like anybody else. Be yourself, even if you feel it's not as good as someone you admire.

As a singer, I didn't make a transition to musical comedy. I just do both. I started doing musicals in Britain, in the fifties, and I think the reason for my longevity in the business is I never wanted to specialize or imitate. I didn't go see *Into The Woods* with Bernadette Peters before I did it 'cause I thought if I did, I'd pick up on what she was doing.

You have to do your own thing. You have to be unique and know in your heart that this is the only thing you want. Knowing that, go for it.

CLEO LAINE

Cleo Laine, world-renowned Grammy Award-winning vocalist, began her London acting career in 1958 at the Royal Court Theatre in *Flesh To A Tiger*, directed by Tony Richardson. Her other British stage work includes *A Midsummer Night's Dream, Women Of Troy, Valmouth, A Time To Laugh,* directed by Tyrone Guthrie, the title roles in *Hedda Gabler* and *Colette*, and Julie in the highly acclaimed 1971 revival of *Show Boat.*

In 1986, Cleo starred on Broadway as Princess Puffer in the Tony Award-winning musical *The Mystery Of Edwin Drood*, for which she received a Theatre World Award and Tony and Drama Desk nominations. Other American stage work includes Michigan Opera Theatre's *A Little Night Music*, Houston Ballet's *Lady In Waiting*, and Lehar's *The Merry Widow* in Detroit.

Her American television appearances include *The Muppet Show; An Evening At The Pops; Live At Wolftrap; Happy New Year, America; Grammy Lifetime Achievement Awards*; and *The Tonight Show*. In 1988 RCA Victor released the critically acclaimed *Cleo Sings Sondheim* album.

STEVE LANDESBERG

"You have to be out there, anywhere, doing your thing."

Steve Landesberg

I was kind of "closet" funny as a kid. I was only funny with close friends, people I was comfortable with. Otherwise, I was shy. But I loved to do characters. I would imitate the people I knew. That's how I got my first job. I played a Viennese violinist on *The Paul Sands Show*. You know how hard it is to do a "cold" reading, so I thought of my friend's father, who was from Vienna. I imitated him and that's how I got the part. I never studied accents or dialects. I just do them by mimicking people. To me it's just fooling around, like I did with my friends.

I went to DeWitt Clinton High School in the Bronx, New York, and grew up near Yankee Stadium. When we used to hang out by the school yard, I would do my "bits" and impressions. I knew I was funny when I made my friends laugh. But I wanted to be an actor.

Bill Cosby had an open audition at "The Bitter End" in Greenwich Village. I read about it in the *New York Post*, as did hundreds of other comedians who showed up. We were told to do two or three minutes. Now, you know people in show business don't listen, so they went on and on. By the time I got up, no one was there to see me, but it led to my doing showcases, without pay. I joined a comedy group called "The New York Stickball Team." We played "The Improv" the same time David Brenner, Jimmy Walker, and Bette Midler did.

We eventually got on *The Ed Sullivan Show* and bombed, but the rejection wasn't too bad 'cause with a group, you share the grief.

I got on *The Barney Miller Show* without an audition. Danny Arnold saw me play the Viennese violinist and said, "Gee, that guy is funny. Too bad he's German." When he found out I didn't really talk that way, he hired me as a crook. I played a "con" man pretending to be a priest. Then, he brought me back as Sergeant Dietrich. They created the character for me, but I'm not an intellectual like the character was. I just had to be real, as we all had to be on *Barney Miller*.

Of course, the show opened up the world for me. It led to a lot of stand-up comedy, concerts, and commercials. That's how I met my wife. She produced the Ryder Truck commercials I did.

I don't do as much acting as I want to 'cause I'm too fussy.

I turned down a movie, 'cause I thought the script was terrible. But, Ruth Gordon was in it, and that was an experience I missed.

I worked on a TV show a few years ago that was less than good, but I got to work with George C. Scott. That was something I'll never forget. He was so much fun to work with.

I've learned not to worry about failure. And that's the best advice I can give. You have to be out there, anywhere, doing your thing. Showcases, workshops, schools, so someone will see you. Doing stand-up comedy is a great way to be noticed. People are always going and looking. The important thing, though, is to do what you do best. Then maybe you'll be lucky, too, and they'll never guess we're just fooling around.

STEVE LANDESBERG

Steve is perhaps best known for his highly successful run as the erudite Sgt. Arthur Dietrich on the highly acclaimed series *Barney Miller*. During his six years on the show, Steve was honored by his peers with three Emmy nominations. Steve's own sense of humor is very close to that of the character he played every week, a sense of humor so dry that you can't be sure whether he's nuts or just putting you on.

His "off-the-wall" humor, as Johnny Carson calls it, has been seen in his stand up comedy routines on dozens of television shows ranging from *The Tonight Show* to prime time specials. During the past several years, Steve has returned to the concert stage, bringing his unique brand of humor to sold-out performances at concert halls and hundreds of colleges and universities across the country, with such success that he was recently voted the N.A.C.A. Campus Comedy Star.

Steve has appeared in his own network television special *The Steve Landesberg Television Show*, which garnered excellent reviews, and his two sports talk specials *Steve Landesberg/Sports Fan*, were recently shown in over 150 markets across the country. He has just completed his first starring role in the motion picture *Leader Of The Band*, which will be released shortly.

Currently, Steve divides his time between homes around the country on his way to the hundred or so concert appearances he makes each year. When not on the road, Steve continues to look for that one great script that will "knock his socks off." Until he finds it, he will continue to bring his special view of the world and his "overpopulated mind" to concert stages and airports all over North America.

HAL LINDEN

"It only took about eighteen years for me to become an overnight success with Barney Miller."

Hal Linden

I didn't start in the theatre. I was a musician. My beginnings were in the Bronx, which I remember as being quite provincial, unsophisticated, homey and small town, and as difficult as anywhere else. I went off to Manhattan, the "big city" to attend Music and Art High School. It was then I met and saw things that opened my eyes.

My goal in life was to be a successful, professional

musician, and I really achieved that. I played clarinet right through high school, into college and into the army, where I was a bandsman.

It was in the army I kind of started fooling around, doing soldier shows, and that was the beginning. Most people who want to go into the theatre usually know that by the time they're ten years old. It never occurred to me till I was out of college, and at that point, I started studying voice and acting and dancing. I did nothing but study for the next ten to fifteen years. It only took about eighteen years for me to become an overnight success with *Barney Miller*.

My career was pretty much predicated in New York City and in the theatre. I did one TV pilot in New York and one in California before *Barney Miller*. I know many actors who have done dozens before getting a "hit."

I had spent the better part of seven years understudying other people. It was a very difficult and painful time of my life. But it paid the rent and kept me in the theatre, and perfected my craft, so I can't really kick about it. Actually, it was an education in itself.

I understudied Alan Alda, Arthur Hill, and some other quite wonderful talents. I watched them and I learned a lot from them. I also made my plans, how I was going to do it different when I "made it." Also, I was building self-confidence. When I was awarded the "Tony" for my role in *The Rothschilds*, I accepted it for all the "understudies" in the theatre.

The first role I actually initiated was in a show called *Something More*, which lasted six days after we got to New York. I replaced Larry Blyden in *The Apple Tree*, got a little part in *Ilya Darling*, and small roles in one play after another. Then I did *The Education of Hyman Kaplan*. The play had a short run, but it was instrumental in my career.

It's not too hard to be great when you get good words. I

think *I'm Not Rappaport* was Herb Gardner's best work of a moderately distinguished career. The role was a "tour-de-force" for me.

Here, as with any role I play, I use my own background and project myself in what I've seen others perform in plays or in movies.

Little bit by little bit, you make a lot of friends along the way. You do what you think is good work, and at least your peers recognize it, even if the public never heard of you. That's how your career is made.

HAL LINDEN

Hal Linden, a native New Yorker, began his show business career as a saxophone player and later toured with the Sammy Kaye, Bobby Sherwood, and Boyd Raeburn bands. As a member of the U.S. Army Band, he became involved in Army revues, which piqued his interest in pursuing a theatrical career. Following his discharge, Linden enrolled at New York's American Theatre Wing. He later studied with Paul Mann and Lloyd Richards.

His first major break came in 1958 when he replaced Sydney Chaplin and starred opposite Judy Holliday on Broadway in *Bells Are Ringing*. That musical was the first of 18 productions in which he appeared. Among his most successful shows were: *On a Clear Day, Wildcat, Something More, Subways Are for Sleeping*, and *Ilya Darling*. In 1967 he starred in *The Apple Tree*, followed by *The Education of Hyman Kaplan* as well as the revivals of *Three Men on a Horse* and *Pajama Game*.

It was his starring role in *The Rothschilds* which won him the Tony and national acclaim, leading to his being sought for the starring role in the TV series *Barney Miller*. After the conclusion of *Barney Miller's* network run, Linden starred in numerous television specials and movies for television before embarking on another popular series, *Blacke's Magic.* Among his earlier television credits are *FYI*, ABC's award-winning public service series; *The Hal Linden Special*; *Hal Linden's Big Apple* and *Animals, Animals, Animals*, a Peabody Award winner. His movies for television include:*My Wicked Wicked Ways, Father Figure, Starflight, The Other Woman, I Do! I Do!* and *The Best of Everything*. He appeared in the theatrical motion picture *When You Comin' Back, Red Ryder?*

Linden, his wife Frances, and their four children reside in Los Angeles. He is a bridge, skiing and golf enthusiast. Linden presently serves as national chairman of the March of Dimes and hosts its annual telethon each June.

CLEAVON LITTLE

"I like people to search to find out who I am. I like to keep the mystery of it all."

Cleavon Little

A wonderful high school teacher in San Diego, Betty Hall, was actually the first one to give me the opportunity to do anything. In 1957, in San Diego, black talents didn't get the chances, but she went past all of that and dealt with pure talent. Then I went to San Diego City College and got the brunt of my training there. Fortunately, under my training, I've always dealt with people who dealt with non-traditional casting, which is what I really believe in; in terms of casting anything, films, television or theatre.

I was well prepared before I came to New York. Then, I won a scholarship to The American Academy of Dramatic Arts. Of course, that was an extra two years of training. But, by the end of the first year, I was working off-Broadway in a show called *Mac Bird*.

Judd Hirsch recommended me for the reading of *I'm Not Rappaport*. I knew Judd for eighteen years. We worked together on *Scuba Duba*. Even after a year and a half of my involvement with the play, I didn't expect to actually do the role and play an eighty-one-year-old man.

I wound up doing it first with Harold Gould in Seattle, and I was supposed to do it with Gabe Dell in New York. Then he couldn't do it, and it was going to be Jason Robards; but it ended up with the real prize winner, Judd Hirsch.

As soon as I put on the old man's clothes, I'm eighty-one years old; but I like people to search to find out who I am. I like to keep the mystery of it all

On occasion, I've had long periods of not doing anything, but in theatre, I've always done what I've wanted to do. I always made the choices of stuff I thought was exciting and different. That's what I think acting is all about.

CLEAVON LITTLE

Cleavon Little starred in *The Emperor Jones* at Pepsico Summerfare and in the film *The Gig*. He made his Broadway debut in *Jimmy Shine* and won the Tony, Drama Desk and Schaffer awards for *Purlie*. Other New York credits include *All Over Town, Resurrection Of Lady Lester, The Great McDaddy, Narrow Road To The Deep North, Scuba Duba, Mac Bird* and *The Naked Hamlet* at the New York Shakespeare

Festival. Regionally he has appeared in *Man Is Man* in the Summerfare, as Oberon in *A Midsummer Night's Dream* at the Los Angeles Shakespeare Festival, as Joseph in *The Charlatan* at the Mark Taper Forum, and as the Narrator in *Joseph And The Amazing Technicolor Dreamcoat* at the Brooklyn Academy of Music.

He starred in the TV series *Temperature's Rising* and has made guest appearances on many series, including an Image Award *Police Story* segment, and movies of the week that include *The Homecoming*, (the pilot for *The Waltons*), *Don't Look Back, The Day The Earth Moved*, and *Denmark Vesey* for PBS. Mr. Little attracted national attention with *Blazing Saddles* and has continued his film career in *High Risk, Greased Lightning, Toy Soldiers, Scavenger Hunt, Vanishing Point, Cotton Comes To Harlem* and *The Salamander*, among others. His most recent films are *Once Bitten*, produced by Samuel Goldwyn, Jr., and Frank Gilroy's *The Gig* with Wayne Rogers. Mr. Little is a graduate of the American Academy of Dramatic Arts.

MARILYN McCOO

"To me, your voice is a muscle. A dancer wouldn't go out on stage without warming up, and I don't think a singer should either."

Marilyn McCoo

When my parents knew I wanted to become a performer, they made sure I was prepared. I had to take voice and dance lessons and music theory classes. The one criteria they insisted on was that I finish school and have a degree. I went to UCLA and got a Business Administration Degree.

Home for me, since I was seven years old, was in Los

Angeles. I started voice lessons when I was twelve years old. That was really a waste of money because I didn't enjoy it then. Actually you shouldn't start training the voice until you're seventeen. My parents didn't know this.

I worked with the same voice teacher at seventeen, for five years, which was great. When I worked with "The Fifth Dimension," we worked night clubs and were doing three shows a night. I was the only one who didn't have vocal problems because my voice was strong enough from the vocal exercises. To me, your voice is a muscle. A dancer wouldn't go out on stage without warming up, and I don't think a singer should either. I start in the shower in the morning with humming exercises. My voice has a very mellow, low quality, and I like to have an edge on it. Coffee gives it that edge. I'll have some just before I go on. I hate tea and honey and lemon. I tried that and I find I spend the rest of the evening trying to kick the honey off my vocal cords.

Of course, "The Fifth Dimension" made everything else possible. I may never have been able to do anything if it wasn't for "The Fifth Dimension" or have met my husband and partner, Billy Davis, Jr.

Although we work together, and apart, my interest in theatre is not his. Theatre is part of the exploration I see for my career and for my growth and for the kind of all around performer I want to be.

I'm really basically somewhat shy; and when I got to play Reno Sweeney in *Anything Goes,* I was able to take liberties I ordinarily wouldn't take. Reno is a character who loved people and loved life. I went for the warmth in her, and like her, dislike phonies and dishonesty. I never saw *Anything Goes* before I did it. Although I had some preconceived ideas about the role, they didn't work, and I had to throw them out and start afresh.

I don't mind taking over a role. It's a challenge to do

something with it that hasn't been done before, trying to make it your own instead of what someone else did. To me that's what's exciting and challenging and hopefully successful. I think truth and honesty in your interpretation is the most important part of it.

I'm enjoying my career so much. I get to "host" a lot. I even took over for Oprah Winfrey on *A.M. Chicago* while she was shooting *The Color Purple*. Although I wouldn't want to do that as a regular job, it's made me a better guest. Now I know how to give an explanation or thought to questions.

I loved working on the soap opera *Days Of Our Lives*, playing a mysterious character. I had to "screen test" for that role, to make sure there was a good chemistry between me and the actor I played opposite.

Whether it's working with *Solid Gold*, or "The Fifth Dimension" or hosting a parade, a benefit, or TV show, or singing with my husband, or doing theatre, I find it's all fun, rewarding and challenging.

MARILYN McCOO

Marilyn McCoo, known for years as the star of *Solid Gold*, served as a host in the historic Live Aid Concert. Marilyn guest-hosted Chicago's popular *A.M. CHICAGO* and Fox Network's pre-Grammy special. Among her most recent television featured performances are *Christmas In Washington, The Constitution Bicentennial*, and *Happy Birthday Hollywood.* Previously, Marilyn has been a featured performer in the Emmy Award winning *Motown Returns To The Apollo, Miss America Pageant, Placido Domingo, Steppin' Out With The Ladies!, Happy New Year America,* and *Tennessee Ernie Ford's America.* Marilyn is seen on the *American Music Awards, The Golden Globe Awards, The Today Show, Good Morning America* and *Entertainment Tonight.*

Among her most recent acting credits is a recurring role on *Days Of Our Lives* and a starring role in *A . . . My Name Is Alice* at the Burt Reynolds Theatre. Marilyn has also guest starred in the ABC movie *The Fantasy World Of D. C. Collins, The Fall Guy, Love American Style, Double Dare,* and *Punky Brewster.* She has completed a role in the feature film *My Mom's A Werewolf.*

Marilyn's early singing career began with the "Versatiles," later to be known as "The Fifth Dimension." After nearly a decade, Marilyn McCoo and husband Billy Davis, Jr., decided to leave the group and establish themselves as a duo. Their first single "You Don't Have To Be A Star" was a number one hit, a certified RIAA Gold million seller and earned them their first Grammy for Best R&B Vocal Performance by a duo. The single boosted their debut album, *I Hope We Get To Love In Time,* on to the charts and to RIAA Gold status as well.

The Marilyn McCoo And Billy Davis, Jr. Show was their reward from impressed network television executives. They headlined in Las Vegas, Lake Tahoe, Atlantic City, and Miami Beach, played to sold-out engagements in Europe and Japan, were awarded the prestigious Grand Prize at the Tokyo Music Festival, and appeared frequently on *The Tonight Show, Dinah, The Merv Griffin Show* and *The John Davidson Show.*

DONNA McKECHNIE

"Sometimes you have to say no and risk and have the courage to wait for or create a role that's really different."

Donna McKechnie

I was seven years old when I started dancing school, and I passionately loved it. My mother realized how serious I was, so she drove me two times a week to school an hour away in Dearborn, Michigan.

When I went to New York, I didn't think it was courageous. I felt it was meant to be. When you're fifteen, you don't know about courage. You think everything is just waiting for you.

And I was very lucky. But when I talk to young people today, I tell them not to be in such a rush to get to New York because every situation is different. I didn't finish school. I had an opportunity to go, so I did it, and lucky for me it turned out all right. But what I see now is so much talent in New York and such stiff competition. There are so many good teachers around the country that I encourage young dancers to stay put and find a good teacher in their hometown. This way, they can compete when they get to New York.

I never stopped my classes. I took drama and voice and directing workshops, too. I guess I'm a professional student. As a chorus dancer, it helps to know the choreographer and have worked for him before. Speaking in a very personal point of view, I never saw myself as a chorus dancer. I never "did it" like anyone else. It wasn't that I was trying to be different as much as that I had a creative urge to interpret in a very personal way. Michael Bennett came to admire this quality and to use it. A lot of my life looks like Cassie's in *A Chorus Line* because of marrying the director, then divorcing him. The similarities are external and superficial.

I don't want this to sound arrogant, because it isn't, but I never understood the kind of person who was happy going from show to show. I don't understand it, but this is what "Cassie" did. I can understand the love of dance, and I know many, many families who were able to live well and put their families through college dancing.

I take it as a compliment when people associate *Chorus Line* with me. But, I think the show is more powerful than any one person. The essence is the definitive story of the life of the "gypsy." And I interpret "gypsy" as anybody who's ever been in a chorus line, going from show to show. Originally, *Chorus Line* was to be a show about dancers, for dancers, based on Michael Bennett's own stories as well as those of hundred's of dancers. It evolved into *Chorus Line* after we listened to the tapes and realized what we had.

After *Chorus Line*, I had to fight the stereotype of Cassie. It's what every performer has to deal with. If you really love creating and want to reach your potential, you have to fight. Sometimes you have to say no and risk and have the courage to wait for or create a role that's really different. You have to constantly prove yourself.

I can't make *Chorus Line* my whole career, but it's so very important to me.

I miss dancing when I don't do it. I've learned never to get out of shape, if I'm ever to do demanding dancing again. I used to think "Theatre" is only New York. But after traveling in the regions like Des Moines or Schenectady, I've learned "they" love good theatre and you can find it everywhere.

DONNA McKECHNIE

Donna McKechnie starred in a new production of *Can-Can* at the West End's Strand Theatre. She received the L.A. Drama Critics award for her role in *Annie Get Your Gun* at the Geary Theatre in San Francisco. She is best known by Broadway audiences for her Tony Award-winning role as Cassie in *A Chorus Line*. She recreated the part in the first English-speaking companies in Paris and Tokyo after her triumphant return to the Shubert Theatre in 1986.

In 1987, the late Bob Fosse cast her in the starring role of *Sweet Charity*, his final production. Other Broadway credits include *How To Succeed In Business Without Really Trying, On The Town, A Funny Thing Happened On The Way To The Forum, Music, The Education Of Hyman Kaplan, Promises, Promises* and *Company*, recreating her roles in the latter two productions in London's West End and Los Angeles, where she was nominated for the best supporting role in a musical.

Ms. McKechnie's regional theatre appearances include

Misalliance, The Threepenny Opera, Call Me Madam, The Apple Tree, Joseph And The Amazing Technicolor Dream Coat, Cabaret, Irma La Douce and *I'm Getting My Act Together And Taking It On The Road*. She has guest starred on TV in *Musical Comedy Tonight III, Show Stoppers, Faerie Tale Theatre, Fame, Cheers* and *Family Ties*, among others. Donna opened Hollywood's Cinegrill Room at the Roosevelt Hotel with her popular nightclub act and has also played the Gardenia Club in Los Angeles, Freddie's Supper Club in New York, and the Plush Room in San Francisco.

CLIFF NORTON

"A lot of stars, and I do mean stars, who became important, have worked their 'buns' off in workshops."

Cliff Norton

I was very lucky. This is the only thing I wanted to do; to be in show business. The first time I got paid for being a performer I was nine years old. I won a talent contest, and my prize was an appearance on a kid's radio show for $8.00.

I didn't have any special training. My training was working. In my day, when I was young, it was a luxury to go to drama school. I didn't even take drama classes in high school. I was too busy with my piano lessons and cutting classes.

Today things are different and I would encourage joining a good group, a good workshop. They're plentiful and a lot are excellent. A lot of young stars, and I do mean stars, who became important, have worked their "buns" off in workshops. Richard Dreyfuss is a good example. We belonged to the same theatre group and met every Monday. Richard was on his feet all the time.

I started out in radio and was a voice actor from the beginning. That's how I earned my living as a teenager, so the transition into doing what we know as voice-overs, commercials, animated stuff, freak voices for cartoons, came easy. A good example was the radio show *Terry And The Pirates.* I was "Connie," the Chinese houseboy. On TV, I was a regular on the *Garroway-At-Large* show handling all the comedy chores with routines such as the "Opera Prompter," the "Dentist" and the "Punch-Drunk Fighter."

I went on to perform on every major variety and dramatic show, including *Ed Sullivan, Milton Berle, Show of Shows, Studio One* and *U.S. Steel Hour*, as well as *Archie Bunker* and *Lou Grant*, to name but a very few. I've always kept busy in the voice-over department with my well-stocked store of character and dialect voices.

In theatre, though, I think the character always has to be close to you. It has to be your true interpretation of that role.

I'm not a student. I'm not a scholar of my profession. I guess I could have been more dedicated. To me the key word in performing always has to be truth. The truth is what has to come out and be transmitted to the audience, so that they'll believe you. This is what I've always attempted and always suggest. Make them believe you.

CLIFF NORTON

Cliff Norton has been active in the commercial field for several years. Among his many credits, he is currently Nick The Grocer, spokesman for Fantastik household cleaner. His well-stocked store of character and dialect voices keep him busy in the "voice-over" department.

He has guested on nearly every TV show originating from Hollywood since he moved out there in 1963, from the *Lucy, Jack Benny* and *Doris Day* days to the present-day *Alice, Archie Bunker, Lou Grant, Eight Is Enough, One Day At A Time*, to name but a very few. TV specials include *It Happened One Christmas* and *Ziegfeld*.

Major motion picture credits: *The Russians Are Coming, Funny Lady, Harry and Tonto, Suppose They Gave A War.*

Norton's experience in the theatre is extensive: Nathan Detroit in *Guys And Dolls*, Luther Billis in *South Pacific*, Heinzie in *Pajama Game*, Ali Hakim in *Oklahoma*, Senex in *A Funny Thing Happened On The Way To The Forum*, Richard Sherman in *Seven-Year Itch*, the Cretin in *Visit To A Small Planet*.

He starred in his very own variety series for the BBC in London and has appeared on British television no less than thirty times.

Commercials now running: Fidelity Federal Bank, Builder's Emporium, Mattel, Lawry's Restaurants, AT&T, Mercedes, Seven-11, Baker Square, Apple Computer, K-Mart, McDonald's, Yellow Pages.

Through the years, he "spoke" for: Tums, Fantastik, Cheer, White Owl Cigars, Allerest, Admiral TV, etc.

EDWARD JAMES OLMOS

"To receive the acclamation for best supporting actor with an Emmy and Golden Globe Award took 25 years of perseverance."

Edward James Olmos

I got my first paycheck in the theatre in 1978, although I started in 1964. So, for fourteen years I didn't get any money for doing theatre. Now, you know what it is to commit to theatre. Even if it's off-off-off-Broadway or community theatre in Butte, Montana, you're participating at their beck and call, usually seven days a week. We end up devoting our life to our craft, with the satisfaction of commitment to the craft. You can't depend on becoming a star or even becoming successful in it. All you can depend on is that you will grow and you'll become a better person inside the craft.

I went to college and studied Sociology, the study of human behavior, which helped me or led me to character acting. I still spend a lot of time looking at people, conversing with people. I've become "the great observer."

Most of the time we learn any way we possibly can. Learning the difference of acting for theatre, television and films can be compared to playing musical instruments. Theatre is electrifying, like an acoustical guitar; television and film, more delicate, like playing a violin. They're all different, but you have to understand the subtleties. Watch television. It's much more subtle. Notice all the close-ups.

Miami Vice was my first series, although I had done TV before. This was my first time in an ongoing situation, and to receive the acclamation for best supporting actor with an Emmy and Golden Globe Award took twenty-five years of perseverance. I have not met any overnight successes. They're there, but they're the minority.

I'm not more talented or smarter than the next actor, but I may be more disciplined. I've continued to work at my craft. It's like a muscle. You have to exercise it.

When it starts off, we're all equal. I wasn't born a singer, dancer or actor; but I've learned by doing it every day, seven days a week, until I got to be pretty good at it. Every day is a learning process for me.

If I started again, I would maybe commit myself sooner. Thirteen wasn't soon enough. I helped support myself working in a "rock and roll" band; and when the opportunity arrived for me to work in the play *Zoot Suit*, I was honored. It was the first American play dealing with Hispanic themes in the history of American theatre. We were commended by the

American Theatre Wing for the commitment to doing this kind of piece, and I got a Tony nomination for my role.

It took till I was thirty-seven to get my first major role and earn enough money to put some in the bank. A lot of my friends were much more talented than I was, than I am today; but even after twenty years, they gave up. They couldn't wait. The reason I'm here today is because I had the patience. That's what it takes, as well as discipline, determination and perseverance.

EDWARD JAMES OLMOS

Edward James Olmos was an Oscar nominee for Best Actor in *Stand and Deliver*, as well as a Golden Globe nominee. He was born and raised in East Los Angeles, graduated from Montebello High, and attended East Los Angeles City College and Cal State L.A. He began his entertainment career in the '60s as the lead singer in a top L.A. band, "Eddie and the Pacific Oceans," which played in the area for seven years.

Olmos was introduced to acting while helping a friend rehearse his part in a play. He then began to actively pursue parts in Equity-waiver productions, supporting himself by delivering antique furniture. His first professional acting job was a small part in the television series *Kojak*. He continued doing episodic television until he attended a cattle-call audition for an Equity-waiver workshop about Latinos. Four callbacks and three months later, Olmos was given the part of El Pachuco in *Zoot Suit*. He would stay with the show for its year-and-a-half run in Los Angeles at both the Mark Taper Forum and the Aquarius Theatre, its eventual move to Broadway, and for its transformation into a film. Olmos' portrayal of El Pachuco won him the L.A. Drama Critics Award, the Theatre World Award, a Tony nomination, and special recognition from the American Theatre Wing as having created one of the "three definitive performances on the American stage."

In 1984, Olmos received a call from producer Michael Mann asking him to join the cast of the hit series, *Miami Vice.* He agreed to play the part of Lt. Martin Castillo, a role for which he has garnered both an Emmy and a Golden Globe Award. Other TV credits include *The Fortunate Pilgrim, Hill Street Blues, Seguin, 300 Miles for Stephanie, Chips, Evening in Byzantium, Wheels Part IV & V, Police Story* (two episodes), *Rafferty, The Fitzpatricks, Faith for Today, Hawaii Five-O, Blue Knight, Starsky & Hutch, Alambrista, Police Woman, Delvecchio, Medical Center, Joe Forrester, Kojak, Bronk* (two episodes), and *Cannon.*

Olmos has also appeared in such films as *Saving Grace, Blade Runner,* and the mini-series *Fortunate Pilgrim.* He has completed a role in *Triumphant of the Spirit,* filmed on location in Auschwitz, Poland. And in 1988, he became one of the few actors to grace the cover of *Time Magazine.* Other films include *Ballad of Gregorio Cortez, Wolfen, Virus, Dead Angle, Hit-Man, Other Side of the Wind, Aloha, Bobby & Rose,* and *Get Fisk.*

JANICE PAIGE

"If I were starting all over again, I'd pay more attention to what God gave me . . ."

Janice Paige

My mother was a woman who could never give expression to her talents and her needs. My father left when I was very young, so she had to support two children. I think I probably ended up with all the attention. You know, people sometimes live through other people. It happens all the time, but I benefited from it.

I was under contract to Warner Brothers for five years.

Although, after that time, they no longer needed my services, they had given me a wonderful name and fame. I was able to go out and work in night clubs and theatres.

Pajama Game was my first show on Broadway. The musical was a classic and gave me great recognition. I've always admired anyone who can get up there and give for two and a half hours. It takes enormous talent and physical stamina.

To prepare, I come into the theatre very early, always. I love to be in the theatre. Maybe, you don't run lines, or you don't work on your role, but there's an atmosphere in the theatre, that just automatically gets me ready. I don't know what it is . . . just a feeling. I vocalize to get my voice warmed up. I think there's a certain technique you prepare for as far as the physical stamina you have to bring to a role.

The offer to repeat a role, to do a play over again is wonderful. That's what happened with me in *Alone Together*. I originated the role on Broadway and three years later got the opportunity to do it at The Coconut Grove Playhouse in Miami, Florida. It wasn't the same play for me the second time. Things changed in my life. Now I had the opportunity to re-think, to correct, to re-feel and re-express.

Some of "me" is always up there. You always bring whatever you are to a role. That's what makes it special. There isn't an actor in the world who doesn't do that. Otherwise, I don't think you're any good. You'd be dull and not truthful if "you" are not up on that stage.

You can't live in this world and not feel things and grow and experience. Now, all those experiences end up on the stage.

Now, I've entered another career. My "late" husband was Ray Gilbert, who wrote wonderful songs like "Zippety-Do-Dah" and "You Belong To My Heart." When he died, he left me The Ipanema Music Corporation, which owns a lot of copyrights, and publishes them. So, I'm really self-taught and I guard it and take care of it very carefully, since I own the whole thing.

If I were starting all over again, I'd pay more attention to what God gave me and what I'd been provided with. I'd be more careful, more selective, and work harder. I've worked very hard, but I'd work harder in different areas. I still don't plan to stop working. I think I'll get a feeling when it's time to stop.

Above all, I love the audience. I always did. I love the people and the strength I get from them and the strength you give them. It comes across, always. Janice Paige isn't "Janice Paige" yet, 'cause I'm always doing, always searching, and trying and won't stop.

JANICE PAIGE

In 1984 on Broadway, Ms. Paige created the role of Helene in the Broadway production of *Alone Together* at the Music Box Theatre and recreated that role at the Coconut Grove Playhouse. Ms. Paige's first starring role on Broadway was in the Russell Krouse comedy *Remains To Be Seen*. Janice went on to even greater success in the smash hit musical *The Pajama Game* and a few seasons later returned to theatre in another musical hit, Meredith Willson's *Here's Love*.

She replaced Angela Lansbury on Broadway in the smash hit musical *Mame*. The talents of multi-faceted Janice are further evidenced by her unique styling of such diversified plays as: *Desk Set, Born Yesterday, Lovers And Other Strangers, The Gingerbread Man, Annie Get Your Gun, Guys And Dolls, Gypsy, Sweet Charity, Company* and the first international company of *Applause* in Johannesburg, South Africa.

Prior to her stage career, she enjoyed wide acclaim for her starring roles in motion pictures beginning with *Hollywood*

Canteen and continuing through a tenure as an exclusive Warner Brothers star. Her numerous film assignments included *Please Don't Eat The Daisies, Bachelor In Paradise, Of Human Bondage, Romance On The High Seas, The Caretakers, Follow The Boys* and *Silk Stockings.*

Bob Hope has presented her on Christmas Specials, and she traveled to many parts of the globe with him entertaining the armed forces in Korea, Guantanamo and Viet Nam. Ms. Paige's guest starring roles on dramatic television include appearances on *Columbo, Police Story, Charlie's Angels* and *Fantasy Island.* Her unique comedic ability has turned up on her own television series *It's Always Jan* and starring with Art Carney in the Mystery Movie Theatre series *Lannigan's Rabbi* as well as on *Alice* and as the role of Dick Van Patten's eccentric sister, Vi, on the long running hit series *Eight Is Enough.* Her most recent television appearances include a regular role on the popular *Trapper John, M.D.*, the daytime soap *Capitol*, and a guest appearance on *Mission Impossible*, which she filmed last December in Australia.

BROCK PETERS

"Fortunately, the audience responds in a lot of ways, but mostly with love."

Brock Peters

I was born in Harlem and grew up in New York. My parents were from different countries, not native born. My mother was terribly interested in my being enriched by the arts. She exposed me early to museums and to the theatre. She insisted on my playing the violin, which I thought wasn't exactly my cup of tea. But, after a while, I found I did like it, and it made it possible for me to get into Music and

Art High School.

It took a lot of training with teachers like Philip Burton, working with very fine actors and directors and a long career with a lot of "on-the-job" training to get me where I am today.

Theater is my first love; and it's a new show for me every night. Each audience is different and they help you authenticate the process that goes on, on stage. If you're a singer, it's fine to sing for a camera and have it recorded. Then it's frozen and that's what it will be always. It's not the personal gratification you get from the live experience as a performer. You know that audience is living and breathing and responding to what you give them.

In a film, after doing the same scene thirty-six times, the audience sees the directors' and the producers' choice, not the actors'.

I'm drawn to "message" plays. Plays that have substance. If I ever got to be considered a household word, it could be said it started with *To Kill A Mockingbird*. In that, as in *Driving Miss Daisy*, I played characters very far from Brock Peters. I like to learn the characters. What are their interests? What are their desires? What is there about them I can reveal? Also, I'm influenced by the ambience, by the setting and by the time, being careful not to overlook what's been given by the author. Very often the clues are right there on the page for us to pick up.

Every day is an education for me. Literally all the characters I've played are from being able to make these observations and having the imagination to make it work.

In *Driving Miss Daisy*, I was taking over a role, once again, that I did not originate. I was allowed to develop with the things I do myself and bring my own technique and talent. I think the play and the production is enhanced in each of the *Daisy* companies this way.

On opening nights, I feel the traditional way, with the concerns and the "butterflies." So, I hibernate; I prepare; I store up energy. I focus my mind and spirit for the best possible performance I can give.

Fortunately, the audience responds in a lot of ways, but mostly with love. That makes it all worthwhile.

BROCK PETERS

Brock Peters was hailed for his performances in the award-laden film, *To Kill A Mockingbird* and also *The L- Shaped Room*. His starring performance in the 1972–1973 revival of the Kurt Weill–Maxwell Anderson musical play, *Lost In The Stars*, brought him a Tony nomination, a Drama Desk Award, and an Outer Critics' Circle Award.

As a producer, he was responsible for the landmark film, *Five On The Black Hand Side*, and the prize-winning documentary, *This Far By Faith*, which was seen on the PBS special, *Voices Of Our People*, winner of ten Los Angeles Emmy Awards.

His career in the theatre began with the role of Jim in a revival of *Porgy And Bess*. Mr. Peters played Jack Jefferson, the towering role based on fighter Jack Johnson, in the national tour of Howard Sackler's *The Great White Hope* and then appeared in Athol Fugard's *Master Harold . . . And The Boys*. He appeared on Broadway in the musicals *Kwamina* and *Body Beautiful* and enjoyed a long off-Broadway run in the title role of *The King Of The Dark Chamber*. He has played Othello on more than one occasion and has often been seen as Joe in *Showboat*.

He appeared in the film versions of both *Carmen Jones* and *Porgy And Bess* and made an indelible impression as Rodriguez in Sidney Lumet's *The Pawnbroker*, opposite Rod Steiger. Among Mr. Peters' numerous other films are *Major*

Dundee, The Incident, Soylent Green, and with Peter Sellers in *Heavens Above!*

The actor's television appearances include *Roots II — The Second Generation, Caribbean Mystery* with Helen Hayes, the series, *The Young And The Restless*, in which he played Captain Lewis, and a recent *Murder She Wrote* with Angela Lansbury. Add to this such recent movies-of-the-week as *Seventh Avenue* and *SST Death Flight*.

Mr. Peters was co-founder (with Arthur Mitchell and Cicely Tyson) of Dance Theatre of Harlem and was the group's board chairman for the first dozen years of its life. He is also a trustee of the new Dance Gallery Complex in downtown Los Angeles and has therefore helped to create major dance institutions on both coasts.

ROBIN RAMSEY

"You're born an actor. You just need the right people to open doors for you."

Robin Ramsey

I was born in Melbourne, Australia. A famous American actress I worked with filming *On The Beach* said, "If you're gonna make a film about the end of the world, Melbourne is the best place to do it."

In school, I was a bit of a dunce, on the academic side of things. Now, in Australia, the "hierarchy" is God, The Queen, The Headmaster, The Prime Minister, then your own father.

So, when the Headmaster said, "This boy is a bit of a dunce. I think he should go into the performing arts," I did. The Headmaster used to do the theatre productions. (This accounts for the high quality of our education.)

I trained at The Royal Academy of Dramatic Arts, which is really a school like any other. But at that time, Australia was suffering a cultural "cringe" in the late fifties, which means we thought anything from overseas was better than our culture, and we had no drama school of our own. The only place to get a job as an actor was overseas, and many of us went. The natural place was London.

Actually, I think anywhere you go as a student, you learn from the one or two teachers that you find appealing, regardless of the structure of the school, whether it's "The Royal Academy Of Dramatic Arts" or "The East End Boys Home."

I did have two fabulous teachers, but you still learn as you go. There used to be a great system of apprenticeship in the theatre that is no more. Soon after leaving drama school, I returned to Australia, and my first job was in the film *On The Beach*. I played an American and had one line. I took the hint and went to New York where I fell in love and married an American girl.

I was cast as the undertaker in the musical *Oliver* and auditioned to understudy Clive Revill as "Fagin." The casting director said, "Sorry, young man, but you couldn't possibly play Fagin; you're only twenty-three." When Clive Revill left the show, there was a new casting director. Playing the undertaker, I looked at least fifty in makeup and costume. The new casting director thought I was perfect, and so I was cast. Fortunately, I was prepared. In Australia, we all do everything. Since it's a small industry and a small place, it helps if you can sing, dance and even juggle.

Australian actors have a feeling of independence which

we gained at some cost, because we were a colony for so long. Australia began not as a rather heroic colony in heroic circumstances, but as a dumping ground for English convicts. So, we've come up the hard way.

As actors, basically, we have to have some aptitude, but some people say, "You're born an actor. You just need the right people to open the doors for you."

I am now "giving back" to those who opened doors, by touring with *Borderland*, a celebration of Rabindranath Tagore, a solo play commissioned by the Government of India. The tour is coordinated by "Global Cooperation for a Better World."

ROBIN RAMSEY

Robin studied at London's Royal Academy of Dramatic Arts in the early sixties, then toured the U.S. with Eva Le Galliene and the American National Repertory Theatre in Tyrone Guthrie's production of *Mary Stuart* and *Elizabeth The Queen*. He demonstrated the versatility which has become his hallmark when at 24 he starred in the original Broadway production of *Oliver* as Fagin. After a run of two years, he recreated the role for the London revival. He appeared on the same bill as the Beatles in a subsequently memorable edition of NBC's *Ed Sullivan Show*.

His musical career continued with Pontius Pilate in Jim Sharman's original production of *Jesus Christ Superstar*, Mack the Knife in *The Threepenny Opera, Rock-Ola*, and *The Sunny South*. His repertoire in the classical theatre is rich and varied with seasons in major companies, particularly in the Sydney Theatre Company. His roles encompass: Pericles, Macbeth, Shylock, Prince Hal, Petruchio (to Diane Cilento's Kate), Richard III, and Polonius in Bogdan Koca's *Hamlet* for the Adelaide Festival in 1986. At the opening of the Victorian

Arts Centre, he played opposite Zoe Caldwell in *Medea*. In the modern theatre, he has appeared in plays from Alan Ayckbourn to David Williamson.

A frequent television performer, he was the dashing Sheikh Amahl romancing Rebecca Gilling in *Return To Eden* and, as a complete contrast, the shy, endearing Wilf Barlow married to Julie Christie in CBS-TV's *A Long Way From Home*.

His Australian feature films include *Mad Dog Morgan, Silent Reach, Oz, Running On Empty*, and Bill Bennett's *Dear Cardholder*. He has narrated many films, notably the award winning *Lempad Of Bali*.

He will tour Europe and the U.S. with *Borderland* in tandem with *Outback Cafe* in support of the United Nations Peace Messenger project "Global Cooperation for a Better World."

FRANCES REID

"Don't go into the theater unless it is the only thing in the world that interests you."

Frances Reid

I got where I am today mostly by LUCK. I just didn't look like the girls of the forties. But I did look right to play in the classics. I had studied at the Pasadena School of Theatre and knew the acting techniques and how to wear the costumes. So I was cast in a number of classics on Broadway: *Hamlet, Cyrano, Twelfth Night, Richard III, The Rivals,* etc. But I also did two flops for George Abbott and lots of other modern flops.

Of course, I worked hard on my voice and speech and physical training. I studied theatre literature and theatre history. But none of that would have got me anywhere without luck . . . and a degree of arrogance. Everybody knows the chances of success in this business are slimmer than winning at the gambling table. But even though I was aware of the odds, I was sure I would win. I have always earned my living through acting.

I'm having a perfectly good time doing *Days Of Our Lives*, as I have been for twenty-three years. Although I often have to rush home to study the next day's script, the character will stay with me. But I'm an actress, and I can leave her any time. In fact, I used to think I've got to do something else, to get away. So, I tried doing a day here and a day there on other shows just for the change . . . but, it was too hard.

Of course, a month shooting *Mercy Or Murder* with Robert Young in 1986 in Miami was wonderful, but different for me.

On *Days Of Our Lives* we work with three cameras, which is wonderful for the actor. We rehearse it and we shoot it. *Mercy Or Murder* was shot like a film, with one camera. It seemed all I did was wait. We waited for them to set up and move everything, for each angle change, only to do it again. But what a wonderful experience. Every line spoken was as it was said. It was done fairly and documented. The audience was left to decide if this man who shot his wife, who was suffering with Alzheimer's disease, deserved mercy or deserved to be charged with murder as he was.

My advice to actors: Don't go into the theatre unless it is the only thing in the world that interests you. The odds of success are so heavily stacked against you. But if you have to do it, study singing, dancing, acting, dramatic literature, and the visual arts.

I've been Alice Horton on *Days Of Our Lives* on NBC since 1965 and never auditioned for the role. I had worked for them before, and that's how casting used to be done. Talk about luck!!!

FRANCES REID

Miss Reid made her professional debut as Helene Du Pont in the West Coast touring production of *Tovarich*. She made her Broadway debut as Juliette Lecourtois in *Where There's A Will*.

In New York City, Miss Reid played Julia in the Theatre Guild production of *The Rivals*; Martha in *The Patriots*; Nina Alexandrovna in *Listen, Professor!*; and Beth in *Little Women*; in the pre-Broadway tryout of *Clover Ring*; as Sally Jones in *Star Spangled Family*; Jean in *The Wind Is 90*; Ophelia in Maurice Evans' *GI Hamlet*; and on tour; Roxanne in the Jose Ferrer revival of *Cyrano de Bergerac*; Minnie in *Rip Van Winkle*; and Elena Popova in *The Bear*; as Gwendolyn in *The Importance Of Being Earnest*; as Ann in Richard Whorf's production of *Richard III*; Viola in *Twelfth Night*; as Judith in Maurice Evans' production of *The Devil's Disciple*; Lady Utterwood in *Heartbreak House*; as Mrs. Antrobus in *The Skin Of Our Teeth*; as Lavinia in *Androcles And The Lion*; as Comtesse Louise de Clerambard in *Clerambard*; as Mlle. de St. Euverte in *The Waltz Of The Toreadors*; as Nora in *A Touch Of The Poet*; Solange in *The Maids*; and Lina in *Misalliance*.

In television, she made her debut in *Charlotte Corday* (NBC, 1939); subsequently appeared on *Prologue To Glory* and *Little Women*; Roxanne in *Cyrano de Bergerac*; as Olivia in *Twelfth Night*; Portia for the series, *Portia Faces Life* (CBS, 1954); Grace Baker in the series, *As the World Turns*; appeared on *Suspense, Danger, You Are There, Cameo Theatre, Philco Television Playhouse, Hallmark Hall of Fame,*

Matinee Theatre, Telephone Time, Alfred Hitchcock Presents, Rose Pollack in the series, *Edge of Night, Wagon Train, Ben Casey, Eleventh Hour, The Defenders, Perry Mason*, and the *Armstrong Circle Theatre.*

Frances Reid has played Alice Horton on the daytime drama *Days Of Our Lives* on NBC from 1965 to present.

CHARLES NELSON REILLY

"I try to give back what I learned by teaching. I realize it makes me happy."

Charles Nelson Reilly

I went to P.S. 163 in The Bronx, New York, and appeared in school plays. I made my professional debut with the Metropolitan Players as the Detective in *Broken Dishes* in Tiverton, Rhode Island, in 1950.

When I was eighteen, I was in a class taught by Uta Hagen. Her fee at that time was one dollar. It was in an awful room in a building that was later condemned. But in this room were Jason Robards, Jack Lemmon, Geraldine Page, Stiller and Meara, Orson Bean, Peggy Cass, Hal Holbrook, Fritz Weaver, Tom Troupe, Barbara Barrie; and everyone became famous. We all had nothing but a mutual admiration for this twenty-six-year-old woman. We stayed for five, six, seven, or eight years. That room has always stayed in my mind. Now I try to give back what I learned, by teaching. I realize it really makes me happy.

What is teaching? Why did Uta Hagen teach? Why do I? You grow up and realize they don't put up a closing notice. It's always there when you want to do it.

Burt Reynolds and I have been friends for over twenty-five years. He opened his theater in Jupiter so he could have a "front" for a school for young people. He appointed me Master Acting Teacher. Everything I learned in Uta's room I shared with those wonderful youngsters. When I direct and get good reviews, I credit Miss Hagen. If I have a house in Beverly Hills, a yacht and a very good car, it's because of what I learned from her in seven years. She's truly an inspiration. She doesn't teach acting; she teaches living.

I got my big break by knowing Robert Morse. He got me an audition for Abe Burrows for *How To Succeed In Business*. I did well and got the part. I was ready and prepared.

Now, when I cast for a play I'm directing, I see everybody. The ones you choose read the best and do the most with what's on the paper. Then they have to be physically right, and available.

I don't act anymore. It's too hard. I want to have fun. My mother was the funniest person in the world, an inspiration. So was Abe Burrows. Right now he'd probably say, "Charles, you were very good, but as usual, you take too long."

CHARLES NELSON REILLY

Mr. Reilly appeared in school plays while attending P.S. 163, the Bronx, New York. He made his professional debut with the Metropolitan Players as the Detective in *Broken Dishes* (Tiverton, Rhode Island, 1950); performed in stock at the Newport (Rhode Island) Casino Theatre (Summers 1950-51); at the Starlight Theatre (Kansas City, Missouri, 1954-60); at the Playhouse-on-the-Mall (Paramus, New Jersey); the Woodstock (New York) Playhouse; and the Matunuck (Rhode Island) Theatre.

He has appeared in the ELT production of *Best Foot Forward*; in *The Saintliness Of Marjory Kempe; Fallout; Lend An Ear; The Billy Barnes Revue* (Carnegie Hall Playhouse, 1959); *Parade* (Players, 1960); in the ELT production of *The Inspector General*; in the three one-act plays, *Three Times Three, The Apollo Of Bellac*, and *Nightcar* (HB Studio, 1956).

Mr. Reilly made his Broadway debut as Mr. Henkel in *Bye, Bye, Birdie* (Martin Beck Theatre, April 14, 1960), and was understudy to Dick Van Dyke as Albert Peterson and to Paul Lynde as Mr. MacAfee, playing their roles 35 times. He appeared as Bud Frump in *How To Succeed In Business Without Really Trying* (1961); and subsequently appeared as Cornelius Hakle in *Hello, Dolly!* (1964).

Since 1962, Mr. Reilly has taught a course in acting for musical comedy and opera at the HB (Herbert Berghof) Studio (NYC).

Mr. Reilly has appeared in the films *A Face In The Crowd* and *Two Tickets To Paris*.

For television: *The Ghost And Mrs. Muir* (Emmy Nomination); *Dean Martin Show; Steve Allen Show; The Match Game; Win, Lose Or Draw; Hollywood Squares*; and host of *Sweethearts*.

As a director: *Private Lives; Belle Of Amherst* starring Julie

Harris; *Paul Robeson* starring James Earl Jones; and *Break A Leg* starring Julie Harris.

As an opera director: *La Boheme; La Traviata; Magic Flute*; and *Die Fledermaus*.

CATHY RIGBY

"I think it's great to have goals and enjoy the process."

Cathy Rigby

I started gymnastics at the age of ten. When I walked into the gym for the first time, I knew this is what I wanted to do. It hit me like a bolt of lightning.

We all have different reasons for starting things, different motivation. I came from a family where there were some problems. There was alcoholism. At the time, I didn't put two and two together, but it was definitely an escape for me. I was extremely shy and very introverted; but when I stepped in the gym, I felt like this is where I belong. This is what I could do well. This is what validated me and gave me my identity.

So with that kind of motivation, I excelled very quickly. I had the body and the talent to do it. All of these things combined helped me make it to the Olympics by the age of fifteen. It really was a lot of hard work and a tremendous amount of preparation that I enjoyed doing and found a great joy in.

I see kids in the playground who play as hard as we work. They run and they jump continually, all day long. If you get that energy channeled into the right thing, you can be good at almost anything. People put limitations on themselves, saying I can't really do it, and they don't even try. But, it's an interesting thing. If you take one step at a time and put one foot in front of the other, learn the basics, then you'll get to the next level, and then the next level. If you enjoy the process, you'll be surprised how far you can go.

I never thought I'd be on stage singing, dancing and acting. I was one of those kids in grade school and junior high who would cry if I had to give an oral book report in front of the class. When I got out of gymnastics, I was offered something in show business for the first time. Now the challenge was there. I thought, if I'm going to compete in this arena, I'd better be prepared. I had the confidence builder of gymnastics and knew if I worked hard, I'd get better.

I was offered a couple of TV episodics, and then *Peter Pan*, in an arena tour fifteen years ago, but I didn't use my own voice. It was all pre-recorded. At that point, I knew it was what I really liked. My voice teachers sat me down the first day and said, "I don't really think we can help you much, but we'll work on it." For the first three years, I didn't hear any improvement, but I loved to sing. I went weekly and practiced about an hour a day. Finally after three years, I heard an improvement. All of a sudden, my breath control was better, and there was some vibrato there. After six years, they said it was time to go out and audition, which was terrifying for me. But I did and got the part. I had to sing "Somewhere Over The Rainbow" in front of three thousand people. Once again, I made the commitment and did it.

Lee and Sally Sweetland, my voice teachers, gave their heart and soul when they taught me. They exude joy and confidence and are so supportive. They have become part of my family.

Now, this is my career and I love it. As long as I can enjoy it, and the audience does, I'll continue.

I think it's great to have goals and enjoy the process and always enjoy whatever it is you're doing.

CATHY RIGBY

Cathy Rigby captured the hearts of millions of viewers during the 1968 and 1972 Summer Olympics and forever changed the course of gymnastics in the United States. The first American woman to win a medal in world gymnastics competition, Cathy went on to win a total of 12 international medals, eight of which were gold.

Although recognized for her athletic accomplishments, Cathy has distinguished herself as a unique talent in the world of acting. She has been performing on stage for the last seven years and has appeared in productions of *Meet Me In St. Louis, Paint Your Wagon* and *The Wizard Of Oz*. In 1986, Ms. Rigby received a Drama-Logue Award for Best Actress for her portrayal of the eternally young Peter Pan. Most recently she starred in a production of *Peter Pan* which toured Vancouver, Seattle and Spokane, and in New York got rave reviews.

Cathy is the mother of four children, two boys and two girls. With her husband, Tom McCoy, a noted producer, actor and singer, Cathy also produces theatrical, television and feature film projects, video-cassettes and special events.

CHITA RIVERA

"I'm a survivor, and I think that's what it's all about."

Chita Rivera

I launched my career at age eleven when I began ballet lessons in my hometown, Washington, D.C. My professional debut was in the chorus, in *Call Me Madam* at age seventeen. I know a lot of people say, "You can never get out of the chorus if you start there." Well, I think the chorus is a state of mind. A lot of people say chorus and they think it's negative. I think you get your best training in the chorus. You get to work with other people. You learn how to give and how to take, how to be "one," and I think that's real important. Otherwise, you have a real selfish person on your hands who says, "let me out there. And it's all me, me, me!!"

In the "olden days," you were either a singer or a dancer. My very dear friend, Lee Becker Theodore, was the original "Anybody's" in *West Side Story* and the creator of *The American Dance Machine*. I'll never forget Lee saying, "They're auditioning for Ben Bagley's *Shoestring Revue*, but you have to sing." I remember her saying, "In no uncertain terms; I am a dancer. Dancers do not sing. Singers sing, dancers dance; so I'm not going." But I said, "Gee, I want to go. I want to see what this is all about." So she said, "Well, then you go." I must say, she was stunned that I did.

Well, I went and I think I sang a commercial, like "Rinso White," or something. I didn't know any songs. I was a nervous wreck. I had never sung, but because I was curious, I went and I got it. I never knew I had a "voice." And, that's what really did it for me . . . Ben Bagley's *Shoestring Revue*. And if I started all over again, I'd do it the same. I'd still be in the theatre as opposed to films.

I've been very lucky. I think you have to have a charmed life. There's a lot of talented people out there who don't get the chance. Look at Shirley McLaine. Carol Haney was out of the show one night, and Shirley went on for her and became a movie star. Carol was just as talented, but that night the right person was in the audience. Who knows, maybe Shirley might have made it anyhow.

I'm a survivor, and I think that's what it's all about. That, and being in the right place at the right time, and . . . being ready!

CHITA RIVERA

Chita Rivera made her professional debut on Broadway in *Call Me Madam.* At age 16, she auditioned for George Ballanchine, winning a scholarship to the School of American Ballet. At 17, she was in the *Madam* chorus. She did a cross-country tour of the musical as a principal dancer, returning to New York to replace Onna White as principal dancer in *Guys and Dolls.* The next year she appeared in *Can-Can.* Her next show was the off-Broadway *Shoestring Revue.* Afterwards, she was given featured roles in *Seventh Heaven* and *Mr. Wonderful* with Sammy Davis, Jr.

Then on the night of September 26, 1957, *West Side Story* opened at the Winter Garden Theatre. Her daughter Lisa was born during this period and the opening of *West Side Story* in London was postponed until Chita could join the company. She played Anita for a year there and returned to the States to co-star with Dick Van Dyke in *Bye, Bye, Birdie.* She was asked to repeat her performance as Rose in the British production, so off she went to London again.

She returned to New York to star in *Bajour,* then toured as Jenny in *Threepenny Opera* and as Charity in the national company of *Sweet Charity.* She played Nicky in the film version. She kept L.A. her home base and returned East to play such diverse roles as Billy Dawn in *Born Yesterday* and Serafina in *The Rose Tattoo.* She also did a tour of *Zorba* with John Raitt. *Chicago* teamed Chita with Gwen Verdon, John Kander and Fred Ebb, and, for a period of five weeks, Liza Minnelli, who replaced an ailing Miss Verdon.

Chita's recent Broadway appearances have been in *Bring Back Birdie* with Donald O'Connor, *Merlin* as the Queen with Doug Henning, her 1984 Tony Award-winning performance in *The Rink,* co-starring Liza Minnelli, and *Jerry's Girls.* Her television credits are numerous and include such recent shows as Showtime's special presentations of *Pippin*, and her own *Chita Plus Three, Broadway Plays Washington! Kennedy Center Tonight*, and The National Theatre of the Deaf's presentation of *The Road To Cordoba*. Chita toured her successful one-woman show in Japan in 1985, and her production of *Chicago* at Harrah's in Atlantic City was a smash hit. Chita's most treasured production is her daughter, Lisa Mordente.

NANCY STAFFORD

"Your attributes and qualities make you more special than anyone else."

Nancy Stafford

I went to college to get a public relations and business degree. I did visit a South Florida talent agent who said, "Don't quit college," after viewing a few snapshots I brought with me. But, I was encouraged to try out for the Miss Florida pageant. I did, and I won the title. I was hosting a pageant during my "reign," and an actor in the audience came up and said, "You're really good at this. You should do commercials."

He introduced me to a few agents and told me to take classes. I was twenty-four years old when I started. Many thought I was too old. But I was immediately successful in commercials and "print" modeling.

But after a year and a half, realizing I needed more training, I went to New York to study. I enrolled in The Stella Adler Conservatory and really worked hard. I also took voice and dance lessons. I knocked on agent Eileen Ford's door one day. She recognized me from my commercials, liked my modeling book, and signed me. The second audition she sent me on was for the now defunct "soap opera," *The Doctors*, and I got the part. It was a great role; a dual role, actually. I played myself and my own mother, who was a "femme fatale."

When *The Doctors* ended, ABC flew me to Los Angeles to screen test for pilots for the 1982 season. I tested for five, none of which I got. But it gave me the confidence to relocate to Los Angeles. I did get some guest shots on several TV series. Then I auditioned for Joan Halloran of *St. Elsewhere*, which I got and played for two years. Eventually, I was written out, but went on to a movie of the week, Disney's *Last Electric Knight*, which led to the series *Sidekicks*. Under Disney's new Hollywood Studio System, I was signed along with Bette Midler, Shelly Long, Danny DeVito, and Tom Hanks. I'm honored to be in such prestigious company. When I was offered the role of Michelle Thomas on *Matlock*, starring Andy Griffith, Disney agreed to suspend and extend my contract.

Kids come to me a lot for advice. I would never say, "Don't go into this business." Lauren Hutton was turned down by every agent till she went to Eileen Ford. Each actor may have a quality that you don't see, that a camera picks up, or an audience may love. Today, they're looking for so much more than the conventional looks of the time. There are so many interesting things that make us special. This is a personality business. You can convince them there's something special about you, that the thousands they've already seen don't have. Of course, models have to be a certain height, slender body, and (certain) bone structure.

I find the more you know, the less you know. I wish I'd started earlier and had more theatrical training when I started. Now, I must study. I've taken soap opera classes, Stella Adler's technique class, and I've studied with Gordon Hunt in L.A. (I highly recommend Max Gartenberg in New York as a teacher. He's a psychotherapist as well, and gets into behaviorism, offering other avenues to explore.)

I suggest you filter through everything your teachers say and apply it accordingly, along with what you bring as an individual out of the things you've learned all your life. Your attributes and qualities make you more special than anyone else.

Learn the business aspect of this business. Learn self-promotion. I knocked on doors and made phone calls from nine to five. I never waited for the phone to ring. I believe in "out of sight, out of mind." This is my business. I get out of bed, get dressed, put on my makeup, and sit at my desk. I take my craft seriously. With training, I've learned to develop a strong self-image and a positive outlook. You can, too!

NANCY STAFFORD

Nancy got a journalism degree at The University of Florida. She won the Miss Fort Lauderdale contest and went on to become Miss Florida in 1977. Her professional career began in commercials, and she is well known as the spokesperson on the "Waterbed City" commercials.

In New York, she studied with Stella Adler and landed the dual role of evil mother and innocent daughter in the soap *The Doctors*. She was cast as Joan Halloran on *St. Elsewhere* and played her for two years. She starred opposite Gil Gerrard in the ABC series *Sidekicks.* Other TV credits include *One Life To Live, Magnum, P.I., Remington Steele, Who's The Boss?, Scarecrow and Mrs. King,* and *Hunter.*

She currently co-stars as Michelle Thomas, opposite Andy Griffith on *Matlock.*

Nancy portrayed Boots Clark in the play *Almost Perfect* at The Burt Reynolds Jupiter Theatre and starred in Noel Coward's *Present Laughter* at The Melrose Theatre in Los Angeles, for which she won a Drama-Logue Award.

JACK STANLY

"My students learned technique. They also learned it's never criticism, it's always correction."

Jack Stanly

I was born in Louisville, Kentucky, to an all-musical family. In fact, my father once operated a gambling boat which plied the Ohio and Mississippi Rivers between Pittsburgh and New Orleans. When I was seven years old, my parents took me to see The Ziegfeld Follies, and I was astonished. From that day on, I was determined to be a part of show business when I grew up.

In boarding school, when I was fourteen years old, we had to take cotillion dance classes. I was a very quick study and very good at it, especially "The Charleston," which was the rage then. I learned it by watching and imitating and embellishing it with my own steps. I won every contest I entered.

I was determined to go to New York and use my new-found success. I talked my parents into letting me go, and I stayed with my sister (who fortunately lived in New York City), all the while studying with many different teachers.

In the "Twenties," it took a lot of courage for a guy to study ballet as I did, which became an integral part of my tap styling.

My big break came when I was signed to understudy Dan Healy in the 1927 production of The Ziegfeld Follies. The stars were Eddie Cantor, Ruth Etting, Irene Delroy, and Claire Luce. Irving Berlin wrote "Shakin' The Blues Away" for me to dance with Claire Foster and Irene Delroy.

Mostly, I enjoyed dancing in the lavish shows which preceded the movies, at the Broadway Theatres like "The Capitol," "The Roxy," "The Paramount," and "The Strand." I was the featured dancer with the stage bands of Glenn Miller, Tommy Dorsey, Jimmy Dorsey, Harry James, and Artie Shaw. When Ginger Rogers made her first appearance at The Paramount in 1929, I was her partner. With Paul Whiteman in the pit, I was the first to dance to "Rhapsody In Blue."

I always continued to study, and as Tommy Nip's apprentice, I discovered my gift for teaching. When Tommy Nip retired due to illness in 1938, I took over his studios.

Over the years, I taught Rita Moreno, Ron Fields, Helen Gallagher, Danny Daniels, Giselle MacKenzie, Janice Paige, Sal Mineo, Christopher Walken, Gloria Swanson, Stanley Doner, Patrice Wymore, Jayne Mansfield, numerous Rockettes, and Gene Kelly. I invented "the barrel roll" turns that

Gene uses in his routines.

Ballanchine sent me his ballet dancers to learn tap, because he thought it was a great way to get them to relax.

Gower Champion did an entire number based on the "pull back," which I developed.

I taught "fighter" Jack Dempsey. Dancing helped with his reflexes.

My students learned technique. They also learned it's never criticism, it's always correction. I've always advised them there's room enough, for you, you, and you.

* * * * * *

Jack Stanly passed away on August 17, 1990.

JACK STANLY

Jack Stanly was known as "The Tap Dance Kid." He was the owner and director of the famous Jack Stanly Professional School of Dance with a normal weekly attendance of 500 students. His was the first Broadway professional school incorporating various dance forms, including tap, ballet, modern, acrobatic and modern jazz.

He has been a regular instructor for Dance Educators, Chicago National, Texas Association, and The Boston Club.

In 1981, Jack received the Dance Scene Publishers Award at the National Dance Masters of America Convention.

In 1989, at the International Dance Convention, with over 1000 dance teachers participating, Jack was selected as one of the ten best in the last fifty years. The other nine selected had studied with him.

He is the creator of the Basic-Tap Dictionary, accepted by Dance Masters of America, Dance Educators.

ALAN SUES

"I think the hardest thing in show biz is the in-between; what you're doing when you're not on stage."

Alan Sues

I always wanted to be an actor. I used to watch the old movies. I got hooked on the old Dorothy Lamour movies, with volcanoes coming up. I'd flood the whole back yard and get the kids to watch. Then we'd have a hurricane.

I was a stand-up comedian for a while, but I was always an actor. I went to the Pasadena Playhouse. My first show was with Miriam Hopkins. On opening night, I bent her back and I thought, gee, if I bent her more, I think we'd get more out of it. So I did the next night, and she bit me right on stage and drew blood. I thought, Gee, showbiz is going to be hard.

And it has been hard, but it's been great. I think the hardest thing in show biz is the in-between; what you're doing when you're not on stage. This is the hardest thing for all actors, so I study all the time. In addition to the Pasadena Playhouse, I studied with Robert Lewis and still study with great teachers.

Of course, the greatest thing for me was *Laugh-In*, a phenomenal TV show. We all worked so terrific together: Ruth Buzzi, Goldie Hawn, Jo-Ann Worley, Lily Tomlin. And you know what? We're all doing theater. Why? Well, for me, I think of opening night of *Tea and Sympathy*, when we got thirteen curtain calls, or of being able to play Professor Moriarty in *Sherlock Holmes*.

When kids ask me for advice, I always say, "Learn your lines before you come to rehearsal." I always do, although a lot of actors won't. When taping *Laugh In*, we'd work from 9:00 a.m. till 4:00 a.m., two days a week. We really had to be prepared. Sometimes we changed clothes twenty-seven times in one day. But we changed into terrific costumes.

Still, I must advise anyone considering this business for a career to think about it very strongly before making a choice. The commitment is not only for when you're lucky enough to work, but for when you're not working, too!

ALAN SUES

Alan Sues last performed on Broadway as Professor Moriarty in *Sherlock Holmes*. His first Broadway appearance was as Ralph in *Tea And Sympathy*. Off-Broadway he appeared in *The Mad Show* for two years and as part of the national company of *Happy Birthday* and *Sherlock Holmes*. He took part in the national tours of *Singin' In The Rain, Sugar Babies* and the concert version of *Sally*.

Mr. Sues' regional, stock and dinner theatre credits include *Peter Pan; The Pajama Game; Play It Again, Sam; How The Other Half Loves; Charlie's Aunt; How To Succeed In Business Without Really Trying*; and others. His most recent theatre credits include roles in *The Three Musketeers, Annie Get Your Gun* and a new play by Elaine May entitled *Matter Of Position*. He has also done his one-man show at colleges and universities throughout the country.

Mr. Sues began his career as a stand-up comedian working at numerous well-known clubs in New York City. His big break came when he was selected as part of the cast of the legendary television series, *Laugh In*, where he remained for five years. Other television appearances included guest spots on *Twilight Zone, Love American Style, Fantasy Island, C.H.I.P.S., The Glen Campbell Show, The Andy Williams Special, Mouth Trap, Hollywood Squares, The Merv Griffin Easter Special*, and 32 other appearances on *The Merv Griffin Show*. Film credits include *The Americanization Of Emily, Wheeler Dealers, Move Over Darling, The Helen Morgan Story, Please Don't Disturb, Oh Heavenly Dog!* and *Smooth Moves*.

LIZ TORRES

"To survive in theatre, I learned to be as versatile as possible."

Liz Torres

I've been in "the business" since I was fifteen years old, and now I'm past forty. I guess I shouldn't tell my age. It does tend to limit you. But, I've survived.

It all began for me in school in the Bronx. The head of the Drama Club had a summer stock company. After meeting him, I knew what I wanted to do for the rest of my life. I went to New York University on a full scholarship, then to the

Actors Studio, and I studied and studied. I even changed my speech. When I was enrolled in public school at age five, I couldn't speak English. They thought I was retarded 'cause I wouldn't talk. They put me in a "special class" 'till my father explained. Now I can hardly speak Spanish.

I learned dialects and accents. I studied with Robert Easton, and he names me in his advertisement in the *Hollywood Reporter* along with Sir Laurence Olivier and Gregory Peck; not bad!!

To survive in theatre, I learned to be as versatile as possible. I studied Italian and Portuguese, opera, and Flamenco dancing. I can twirl a baton and tap dance. There's very little I can't do. I can "call" a show, and I can work a light board. There's no way I'm going to lose a job 'cause I can't do it.

I was cast in a TV western as part of the *Wild, Wild West*. I thought, never in my life would they hire a sophisticated, New York Puerto Rican for this role. They asked me if I could ride a horse. "Can I ride a horse?" I replied. They asked if I could do a Mexican accent. "Can I do a Mexican accent?" I repeated and got the role. In the script, I had to chase a train on horseback, swirling a sword over my head. So I went to this ranch in Los Angeles and learned how to do it. Then, they put me on a buckboard, and I never had to ride at all. Typical!!

I'll gratefully accept any part. Acting is acting, but there is more. There's survival; there's politics; there's accepting what you can't change. I've learned to give them what they want and to do what the director suggests. I've bit my tongue, counted to ten, and never let anger or frustration get in my way.

At Phil Foster's suggestion, I tried "stand-up" comedy. I wrote my own act about being Puerto Rican, about my family, and about school in New York. I started at "The

Improvisation," got one laugh, and was hooked. David Brenner, Richard Pryor, and Bette Midler were there. We'd do stuff together. Eventually, I worked with Billy Eckstein and opened for Liza Minnelli in Las Vegas.

LIZ TORRES

Singer, dancer, comedienne, dramatic actress — beautiful Liz Torres does it all! Liz studied drama and dance in the Liceo Ponceno School in Puerto Rico and at New York University School of the Arts, obtaining scholarships to attain her goal. While dancing in a review in Las Vegas, Phil Foster suggested she try stand-up comedy because she was so funny. Liz soon started writing comedy material for herself. Liz' big break was when she auditioned and subsequently appeared on *The Tonight Show* in New York. Liz' career started to soar, and she was on her way.

Miss Torres appeared at the Burt Reynolds Jupiter Theatre as Aldonza in *Man of La Mancha*. On Broadway, she did the role of Googie Gomez in *The Ritz*. Other stage credits are *Beautiful Mariposa, Bye, Bye, Birdie*, and *A Girl Could Get Lucky*. In New York, Liz starred in *She, That One, He, The Other* for the Puerto Rican Traveling Theatre. Across the country, her night club appearances have been with Liza Minnelli, Tony Bennett, Billy Eckstein, and Helen Reddy, among others. She has also had the honor of giving a command performance for King Hassan II of Morocco.

Liz' film credits include *Poker Alice* with Elizabeth Taylor, *Sunset* with Bruce Willis, James Garner, and Blake Edwards, *Hot To Trot* with Elliot Gould and Bob Gaithwate, *Up The Down Staircase, If We Knew Then, Scavenger Hunt*, and *Moonbeam*. She has delighted audiences as a regular on such television series as *All In The Family, The New Odd Couple, The Comedy Bag, Phyllis, The Ben Vereen Show*, and *Check-*

ing Out. She has guested on *L.A. Law, Duet* (pilot), *Hunter, Murder She Wrote, All The Way Home* (pilot), *Gimme A Break, The Mike Douglas Show,* and *The Merv Griffin Show.* Miss Torres also starred in the Movies of the Week: *Kate's Secret, Murder in Prison,* and *Women In Prison.*

TOM TROUPE

"You have to be instinctive. You're either born with it or you're not."

Tom Troupe

I grew up in Kansas City, Missouri, and did plays all through high school and college. Then I went to New York to study with Uta Hagen and Sherman Marx. I became a protege of Joseph Schildkraut and made my Broadway debut with him in *The Diary of Anne Frank*.

Now, I'm an actor, a director and a teacher. I can't imagine being able to teach and not being an actor, or directing and not being an actor. It kind of fits into place for me. I just think that actors make the best directors. Mike Nichols, who I think is the greatest director we have, was an actor. But I don't think you can teach directing. You have to be gifted that way. You have to be instinctive. You're either born with it or you're not.

A voice teacher I had, Henry Jacoby, taught me something I try to pass on to my students. He always said, "Build strength where strength lies." It seems to me that's a very good lesson, and that's how I work with actors so they'll gain confidence. I came out to Hollywood to test for the film *The Big Fisherman*. I got the role and stayed in California until I went back to Broadway to do the play *Romantic Comedy*. I toured with it, as well as *Same Time Next Year* opposite Barbara Rush.

The brief times I was with the students at The Burt Reynolds Institute for Theatre Training, I asked them to buy what I say, take the strength out of it, add everything they feel, and everything that touches them in any kind of personal way. To use it, nourish it, and then discard anything that doesn't work for them. I wouldn't ask them to buy everything I say.

Teaching does wonders for the ego, but a great teacher leaves the classroom and cuts it off. My problem is that I feel too responsible. I feel it doesn't end for me when the class stops. I mean, I worry if that kid will get a job. A good teacher gives them all he can during those three hours, then stops because it's all over.

Although theatre is my love, I of course do television. It's very lucrative. I don't think there's that much of a difference making the transition to TV, not if you're a good actor. In a way, it's much easier. You don't have to worry about projection, so vocally it's a lot easier.

Rejection is terrible, as you know. It doesn't just end when you're young. It goes on and on. In California, where you're up against fifty people for one role, you're rejected constantly.

Whatever success I've had in this business has come from hard, hard work. I have never gotten a job through a reading. I'm simply not good at "cold" readings, but one play has led to another, one television show has led to another; by people remembering and liking my work and recommending me for the next job. I think the work in itself is the most important element. Good work somehow breeds work.

TOM TROUPE

Tom Troupe made his Broadway debut in *The Diary of Anne Frank*. He co-starred with Barbara Rush in the National and Canadian tours of Bernard Slade's *Same Time Next Year* and in Mr. Slade's *Romantic Comedy* with Karen Valentine. On Broadway, he appeared in the same play opposite Mia Farrow. *SOFI*, the film version of his one-man stage adaptation of Gogol's *Diary of a Madman*, won him the Best Actor Award at the Atlanta Film Festival.

On television, he has guest-starred on all major series, including *Cheers, Cagney and Lacey, Highway to Heaven*, and *Mary Hartman, Mary Hartman*, in which he played the role of the dotty psychologist, Bob Gilroy. His directing credits include *The Supporting Cast, Father's Day*, and *Patio/ Porch*, all starring his wife, Carole Cook. Mr. Troupe appeared several times at the Burt Reynolds' Jupiter Theatre in Florida and was on the faculty of Mr. Reynolds' Institute for Theatre Training.

ELI WALLACH

"The big secret to me in acting is to really listen to what someone is saying and to be relaxed."

Eli Wallach

I started training at The Neighborhood Playhouse as a student of Sanford Meisner and Martha Graham. We learned a lot about body movement, which I think is a very vital part of performance. It's a kind of "shorthand" of communicating.

I'm an original member of The Actor's Studio, which started in 1947 and is still running.

Clifford Odets was a member and wrote for them. I auditioned for his play *The Country Girl*, and he said, "No, no, no. I'm looking for a romantic leading man." I said, "Well, my wife is four months pregnant, and I'm feeling very romantic." I didn't get the part. I met my wife, Ann Jackson, at Equity Library Theatre. It was is a great place to showcase ones "wares."

Bobby Lewis directed for The Group Theatre, which delved into scenes of realism. Bobby was the one maverick in the group who said, "No, I believe in style. Acting in theatre is make-believe; it isn't real." That's how he directed me in *Teahouse Of The August Moon* and in *The Flowering Peach* by Clifford Odets.

In the first movie I made, Karl Malden said to me, "Don't open your mouth too wide, they'll see your fillings and your tonsils." So, I spoke through closed lips. The director said, "I don't want the Japanese version. Open your mouth."

We must learn not to overdo in films. A different set of muscles are used. The big secret to me in acting is to really listen to what someone is saying and to be relaxed. If you're relaxed, it really comes quite easily; but that's the hardest thing to do. There are certain exercises. Stanislavski worked with Opera Singers, who used florid gestures. He told them they didn't always have to punctuate with their hands and tied their hands to prove it.

God always leaves out one element in a person. He'll take someone who's beautiful and perhaps they'll lack humor, although they may be perfect in many ways. Some people don't have a funny bone in them. I find comedians are not usually funny in person; in fact, they're rather sad.

Some people say acting can't be taught. I think talent can't be taught, but acting is a skill or a technique that can be taught. Exercises can be done. You can soon learn how to concentrate on a stage, how to talk, and how to listen in a play.

Just don't let anyone discourage you, if you really believe you want to be what you want to be. Enough people will try to discourage you in your intentions and your desires and your hopes, so don't discourage yourself. Get a good ground in education. There's a lot out in the world beside the theatre. Learn about politics, about art, about music. Go to museums and go to school.

I'm often asked, "Did you encourage your children to go into the theatre?", as if they were saying, "Would you push your children off a cliff?" I think if they're hooked on it and want to do it, it's their one trip through life, and they should do it. One of the secrets of longevity is interest. Keep at it, keep at it. You can't ever solve the human dilemma and that will keep you going.

ELI WALLACH

Eli Wallach made his stage debut — and met his wife Anne Jackson — in an off-Broadway Equity Library Theatre production of Tennessee Williams' *This Property Is Condemned.* A leading interpreter of Williams' work, he appeared in *The Rose Tattoo*, for which he received Tony, Theatre World, and Donaldson awards, and also appeared in Williams' *Camino Real*, directed by Elia Kazan.

He appeared on Broadway with his wife in Murray Schisgal's comedy *Twice Around The Park*, which they also performed at the Edinburgh Festival; *The Typist And The Tiger* (directed by Arthur Storch); *Major Barbara; Rhinoceros; Luv; Waltz Of The Toreadors*; as well as the off-Broadway production of *The Diary of Anne Frank* and at the Public Theatre in *The Nest Of The Wood Grouse*, which also played in the Eisenhower Theater. He also appeared in *Henry VIII, Mr. Roberts, Alice In Wonderland, The Cold Wind And The Warm, Staircase, Every Good Boy Deserves Favor*, and the

London and New York productions of *Teahouse Of The August Moon*. He toured with Katharine Cornell in *Antony And Cleopatra*, in Ayckbourn's *Absent Friends*, and John Guare's *House Of Blue Leaves*.

For his first film, *Baby Doll*, he won the English equivalent of the Academy Award. Since that time his film career has included *The Magnificent Seven; How The West Was Won; Lord Jim; The Moonspinners; The Good, The Bad, And The Ugly; How To Steal A Million; The Deep; Cinderella Liberty; Movie, Movie; The Hunter; Girlfriends*; and the film *Nuts* with Barbra Streisand and Richard Dreyfus. With Anne Jackson he has performed on screen in *How To Save A Marriage And Ruin Your Life, Zigzag* and *The Tiger Makes Out*.

He has also appeared on television in such specials as *Skokie* with Danny Kaye; *The Wall, 20 Shades Of Pink, Saturday, Sunday, Monday*, Mailer's *The Executioner's Song* and Odet's *Rocket To The Moon*. Born in Brooklyn, he studied at the University of Texas and holds a Master's Degree in Education from New York's City College. He began his training for the theatre at the Neighborhood Playhouse. A charter member of the Actor's Studio, he loves tennis, photography, clock collecting, and architecture.

MORE WISE WORDS FROM THE STARS

KAYE BALLARD

I started in this business when I was fifteen years old, and I've been in it for forty-five years. As Phil Silvers said in *Top Banana*, it's taken me twenty years to become a star overnight.

It's perseverance and sticking to it and having to pay the rent that got me here.

You can have one hit song or get a part in a TV series today and literally become a star overnight. Yeah, TV has ruined everything.

DAVY JONES

You find out about acting by acting, and you must be willing to travel, 'cause you can't be a "hit" on your own back doorstep. Make goals and even if you don't accomplish them, there's nothing wrong in trying. I had four goals: to walk on a tightrope, to ride a camel, to run a marathon, and to make a million dollars. I've done them all.

Booker T. Washington said, "Success is not to be measured by the position you reach in life, but by the obstacles you overcome to reach that success." I say, "The door to opportunity is marked push!"

Davy Jones offers many more quotes in his book *They Made A Monkey Out Of Me.*

LARRY KERT

If you're going to make a mistake, make a big one, then you can pick yourself up, dust yourself off, and start all over again. I never took a singing lesson before I was cast as Tony in *West Side Story*. I was a natural talent and thought I could get away with murder until Leonard Bernstein came to me and said, "You're not sustaining on any of the songs and you need help." I took his advice and started studying and still do. And you should, too.

MARCIA LEWIS

Everything I've done in night clubs has always been like a huge audition, showing I'm somebody who can play a variety of parts, and it worked. I got a TV series (although it didn't last very long).

Funny, talented people who can sing could put together a Cabaret Act to showcase. You just have to do it in the right place. If you're after TV, it's California; if it's theatre, New York is the place.

It might even start a whole new career, and you get paid for it.

GAVIN MACLEOD

Students always ask me, "How do I become a star?" I always answer, I don't know about that, but I can tell you how to become an actor. You keep doing it and you go to school all your life. Some of the very best actors were in my classes in New York, but couldn't make the next step. They couldn't audition. They couldn't deal with rejection.

I was in a play when I was four years old. I heard that applause and said, "I want more of that, and it's all I've wanted to do." It's the applause that keeps me going. If I don't do a play every two years, I'm missing something. It's a shot of adrenalin. With *Love Boat* I saw the world and got paid for it, but it was my theatre training that makes me ready on the first or second take.

Theodore Roosevelt used to say, "Give me a man who tries and fails, rather than the man who doesn't try at all."

DONALD O'CONNOR

First, read the script to see what the author is saying. It's his words, not yours. I always try to find a role model. In *Showboat* for Captain Andy, I thought of Walter Houston, most of the time. I know I don't look like him or talk like him. It's an attitude and can work for every part you play. I even use "attitude" when I'm dancing. With Gene Kelly, I adapted his style for *Singing In The Rain*, and I like to think it helped make the film a classic.

MILO O'SHEA

I began as a "boy" actor in Dublin and made my Broadway debut in *Staircase*, for which I got a "Tony" nomination. I've always felt drawn to musicals though, because they seem to run longer.

I like to mix theatre with film and TV. One must learn the technique of working for film. Stage actors used to "poo poo" that, saying the camera must adjust to them, but that isn't so.

Learn how to play for the camera, to broaden your performance for the long shot, hold back for the close-up, and pray they'll let you bring your own style to the character. If you don't have a "style" as yet, keep training till you acquire one.

Mr. O'Shea recently starred in *Meet Me In St. Louis* on Broadway.

PATRICK QUINN

I got bitten by the "show-biz bug," seeing shows "on trial" in Philadelphia, where I grew up. I did as many shows as I could in high school, and being cast there in *Fiddler On The Roof* and eventually doing it in New York really got my career going.

I trained for theatre, which really was a tremendous help in my getting commercials. I used to walk into an audition and see all these gorgeous men and be so intimidated, but I'd get the job, 'cause I could act.

I saw an interview with Paul Newman, where he said, "How many people like their jobs so much, they'd do it for free?" That kind of says it all.

TOPOL

The army decided I'd make a better entertainer than a soldier. An officer overheard me telling jokes, and I got the order to join the Army Theatre and that's how my career began.

In Israel we have very few actors out of work, 'cause if an actor doesn't find work in three or four years, he tries something else, unlike the actors in England and the United States.

Tevye and *Fiddler On The Roof* have been an important part of my career. Although Tevye could have been my grandfather, I'd like to believe that even if I didn't know this character so intimately, that with research and training, I'd come up with a complete part.

Once you're on stage, when the lights come on, and the curtain is up, it doesn't matter if you play on the West End in London, or Broadway in New York, or in the Army Theatre; an audience is an audience is an audience, and an actor is an actor is an actor!

WILLIE WATERS

Maestro Willie Waters is the Artistic Director for The Greater Miami Opera.

Conducting is an athletic activity for which you have to prepare. You stand in front of a mirror, and you beat time. You beat the patterns, and you work on your technique, because any performance art, whether you're a singer or a conductor, is a science first and then it's an art. In other words, you get the technique down; you know what beat pattern you need to lead the orchestra and the singers. You know how to use your hands, your arms, your face, and your body.

I encourage young artists to experience things and to try things and to take some chances.

If you want to conduct, you have to recognize if you have the talent. Are you a leader and do you have communication skills?

Then you study. You study scores; you listen to recordings; you study composition; you study theory. You've got to know as much or more as all the musicians put together. You've got to know history and performing styles and art. Any way you look at it, it's an enormous task; but, oh, so very rewarding.